ENGLISH 8

FOR YOUNG CATHOLICS

WRITTEN BY
SETON STAFF

SETON PRESS
FRONT ROYAL, VA

Executive Editor: Dr. Mary Kay Clark
Editors: Seton Staff

© 2013 Seton Home Study School
All rights reserved.
Printed in the United States of America

Seton Home Study School
1350 Progress Drive
Front Royal, VA 22630
Phone: (540) 636-9990
Fax: (540) 636-1602

For more information, visit us on the Web at: www.setonhome.org
Contact us by e-mail at: info@setonhome.org

ISBN: 978-1-60704-118-4

Cover: *Blessed Mother Meditating* by Cope

Back Cover: Brompton Oratory, London, England.

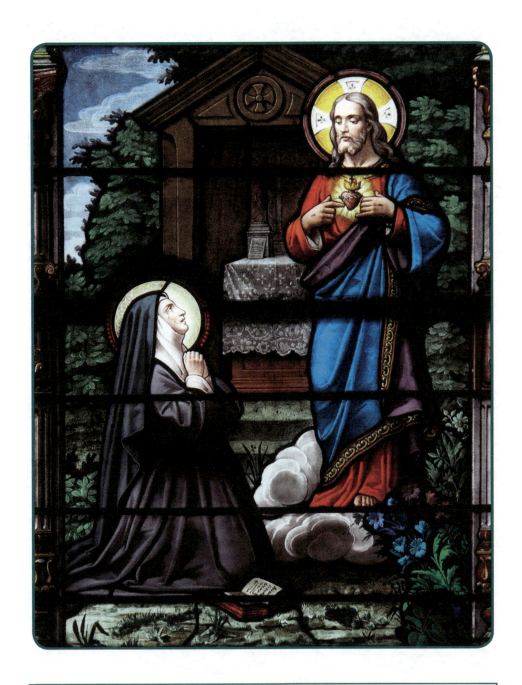

DEDICATED TO THE SACRED HEART OF JESUS

Contents

CHAPTER 1 NOUNS ... 1

Types of Nouns: Proper, Common ... 4
Kinds of Proper and Common Nouns: Collective Nouns ... 5
    Abstract Nouns and Concrete Nouns ... 6
Qualities of Nouns: Person ... 7
    Number ... 8
    Gender ... 11
    Case ... 12
    Case: Nominative: Subject ... 14
    Case: Nominative: Subjective Complement ... 15
    Case: Nominative: Direct Address ... 16
    Case: Nominative: Appositive ... 17
    Case: Nominative: Exclamation ... 18
    Case: Nominative: Review ... 19
    Case: Possessive: Rules for Forming ... 20
    Case: Possessive: Separate and Joint Possession ... 22
    Case: Objective: Direct Object ... 23
    Case: Objective: Cognate Object ... 24
    Case: Objective: Objective Complement ... 25
    Case: Objective: Adverbial Objective ... 26
    Case: Objective: Indirect Object ... 27
    Case: Objective: Object of a Preposition ... 28
    Case: Objective: Appositive ... 29

CHAPTER 2 PRONOUNS ... 31

Personal Pronouns ... 35
    Person, Number, and Gender ... 36
    Case: Nominative ... 37
    Case: Objective ... 39
    Use with *Than* and *As* ... 41
    Compound Personal Pronouns (Reflexive and Intensive) ... 43
    Possessive Pronouns ... 45

Contents

Demonstrative Pronouns 47
Interrogative Pronouns 49
Relative Pronouns..51
Indefinite Pronouns 53

CHAPTER 3 ADJECTIVES 57

Kinds of Adjectives: Descriptive..61
    Descriptive: Position 62
    Limiting: Articles and Numerals..63
    Limiting: Pronominal 64
    Limiting: Pronominal: Demonstrative 65
    Limiting: Pronominal: Possessive 67
    Limiting: Pronominal: Interrogative...69
    Limiting: Pronominal: Indefinite 70
Degrees of Comparison of Adjectives 71
Correct Use of Adjectives: *Fewer* and *Less* 75
    Repetition of the Article 76
Words Used as Adjectives and Nouns 77

CHAPTER 4 VERBS 79

Verbs and Sentences..82
Verb Phrases..83
Kinds of Verbs According to Form: Regular..84
    Irregular..85
    Irregular Verbs: *Lie* and *Lay*, *Rise* and *Raise* 89
Kinds of Verbs According to Use: Action Verbs: Transitive, Intransitive 90
    Being and State of Being Verbs (Linking Verbs) 92
Qualities of Verbs: Voice..94
    Tense: Simple 96
    Tense: Perfect 98
    Mood..100
    Mood: Indicative 101

CONTENTS

    Mood: Indicative: Emphatic, Potential, Progressive 102

    Mood: Imperative 104

    Person and Number 105

Subject/Predicate Agreement 106

    Compound Subjects: *And* 108

    Compound Subjects: *Each, Every, Many A, No* 109

    Compound Subjects: *Neither/Nor, Either/Or* 110

    Collective Nouns 111

Words Used As Verbs and Nouns 112

CHAPTER 5 ADVERBS 113

Adverbs 116

Kinds of Adverbs: Time, Place, Manner, Degree 117

    Affirmation and Negation 119

    Interrogative 120

    Adverbial Objectives 121

Degrees of Comparison of Adverbs 122

Correct Use of Adverbs and Adjectives in Sentences 125

Correct Use of Adverbs and Adjectives after Linking Verbs 127

Correct Use of *Farther, Further,* and *Equally* 128

CHAPTER 6 PREPOSITIONS, CONJUNCTIONS, INTERJECTIONS 129

Prepositions: Definition and Function 132

Words Used as Prepositions and Adverbs 135

Correct Use of Prepositions: *Between/Among, Beside/Besides* 136

    In/Into, From/Off 137

    Differ With/Differ From, Angry With/Angry At 138

Prepositional Phrases: Adjectival and Adverbial 139

Conjunctions: Definition and Functions 140

Kinds of Conjunctions: Coordinate and Correlative: Words and Phrases 141

    Coordinate: Independent Clauses 143

Contents

    Subordinate Conjunctions: Dependent Clause, Independent Clause 145
    Conjunctive Adverbs 147
Correct Use of *Like/As, Like/As If*..149
Interjections 150

CHAPTER 7 CLAUSES AND SENTENCES 151

Clauses: Independent and Dependent 154
    Dependent: Adjective Clauses 156
    Dependent: Adverb Clauses 158
    Dependent: Noun Clauses 160
Sentences: Essential Elements 164
    Natural and Inverted Order 166
    Types According to Use: Declarative, Interrogative, Imperative, Exclamatory 167
    Types According to Form: Simple, Compound, Complex 168
Run-On Sentences and Sentence Fragments 170

HANDBOOK 171

CREDITS 181

ANSWER KEY 183

Introduction

This book is the result of hours of work by many people who want you and your children to learn about the English language as well as to learn about our Catholic heritage. Seton is publishing its own Catholic series, the lessons being modeled after the excellent series once used in Catholic schools.

This book is written for our eighth graders, most of whom already have had some English grammar through our program. If your child has had little or no grammar, you may wish to go back to the sixth or seventh grade level before using this workbook.

Students enrolled in Seton's eighth grade will be covering this book in one semester. We advise families, whether enrolled with Seton or not, to take the necessary time to help the student to learn the concepts. Some students may need to take a whole school year to work on these lessons. It is important for the student to slow down and learn the material rather than rush ahead into high school without these lessons. We include the answer key in the back of the book.

We include diagramming in this text-workbook. We encourage you to give your child diagramming exercises in addition to those presented. Diagramming forces children to think of concepts and relationships.

The key to learning anything is review. It is even more important in English since the lessons build on previous concepts. We encourage you to spend ten to fifteen minutes in reviewing past concepts before proceeding to the new lesson for the day. If you are short on time, it would be more important to review than to proceed to the new concept without review.

Those of us who learned English in the parochial school classrooms with the young nuns for teachers in the forties, fifties, and sixties, grew to like the challenge of English. We thought diagramming was fun and looked for more and more complex sentences to challenge us at the blackboard. English was the pride of the Catholic school system.

We hope you and your children take pride in the challenge and joy in learning English, a real jewel in the heritage of American Catholic education.

CHAPTER 1

NOUNS

NOUNS

NOUNS

Chapter Outline

CHAPTER ONE

I. **Types of nouns**
   A. Proper nouns
   B. Common nouns

II. **Kinds of proper and common nouns**
   A. Collective nouns
   B. Abstract nouns and concrete nouns

III. **Qualities of nouns**
   A. Person – first, second, third
   B. Number – singular, plural
   C. Gender—masculine, feminine, neuter
   D. Case
      1. Nominative case
         a. Subject
         b. Subjective complement
         c. Direct address
         d. Appositive
         e. Exclamation
      2. Possessive case
         a. Rules for forming the possessive case
         b. Separate possession and joint possession
      3. Objective case
         a. Direct object
         b. Cognate object
         c. Objective complement
         d. Adverbial objective
         e. Indirect object
         f. Object of a preposition
         g. Appositive

Lesson 1

NOUNS

Types of Nouns—Proper Nouns and Common Nouns

> A **noun** is the part of speech that names a person, place, or thing.
> A **proper noun** is the type of noun that names a particular person, place, or thing. Proper nouns always begin with a capital letter.
> A **common noun** is the type of noun that names any of a class of persons, places, or things.

Examples:

Proper Noun	Noun names a	Common Noun	Noun names a
Senator Mitchell	particular person	senator, legislator, candidate	class of persons
Bishop Walsh	particular person	bishop, pope, priest, clergy	class of persons
Milwaukee	particular place	city, town, state, world	class of places
Isle of Capri	particular place	hemisphere, tropics, seashore	class of places
Holy Cross Church	particular thing	church, cathedral, shrine	class of things
Lipton Tea	particular thing	beverage, refreshment, party	class of things

Exercise 1: Circle the proper nouns and underline the common nouns in each sentence.

1. God created Adam and Eve, our first parents.
2. Jesus chose twelve simple men to be apostles.
3. Gabriel, an angel, asked Mary to be the mother of Our Lord.
4. Jesus Christ died for our sins and to make us children of God again.
5. John, the cousin of Jesus, baptized believers in the Jordan River.
6. St. John reluctantly baptized Jesus in the river.
7. A pilgrimage through the Holy Land is a touching experience.
8. The priesthood is a special vocation.
9. The youth choir at Holy Redeemer Church is well-known throughout the state.
10. The choir performs every Sunday and on special feast days.

NOUNS

Lesson 2

Kinds of Proper and Common Nouns: Collective Nouns

> A **collective noun** denotes a group of persons, animals, places, or things considered as one. Collective nouns may be proper or common.

Examples of Collective Nouns

assembly	herd	choir	team	collection
parish	fleet	swarm	multitude	community
class	set	U. S. Congress	U. S. Navy	Minnesota Orchestra

Exercise 2: Circle the collective nouns in each sentence.

1. The congregation listened to the words of the homily.
2. Our altar boys' club has many exciting activities.
3. The Immaculate Conception Society received special attention from the pope as he passed by.
4. The crowd listened quietly as the orchestra played music for the Holy Father.
5. The audience applauded when the band finished the song.
6. All mankind should listen to the words of the Holy Father.
7. Several professional football teams belong to the National Football League.
8. In our country, a person is presumed innocent until proven guilty by a jury of his peers.
9. The community of priests lived near the Holy Father in Rome.
10. The Confederacy of American States was formed during the Civil War.
11. Buffaloes once roamed the plains in large herds.
12. Bishop Welch addressed the congregation every Sunday in Lent.
13. A board of volunteers meets on the third Thursday of every month.
14. The captain of the steamship praised the crew.
15. Every bishop is a shepherd of his flock.

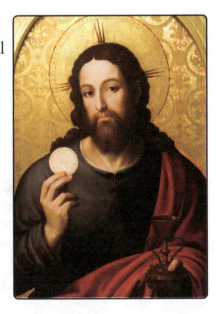

Saint Thomas More, Pray for us!   J.M.J.   English 8 for Young Catholics   5

Lesson 3: NOUNS

Kinds of Proper and Common Nouns: Abstract and Concrete Nouns

> An **abstract noun** names a thing that is a quality or condition.
> A **concrete noun** names a person, a place, or a thing that exists in a material or physical form.

Abstract nouns *honesty, power, happiness, friendship, motherhood*
Concrete nouns *bishop, restaurant, sandwich, bridge, paragraph*

> The distinction between an abstract noun and a concrete noun is not always clear. For example, *sunshine* or *morning* may be considered abstract or concrete, depending on one's point of view. What is important is being able to identify nouns in a sentence.

Exercise 3: Underline all the nouns in each sentence.

1. Mother Teresa brought sympathy to the poor and encouragement to the sick.
2. To receive Christ daily in the state of grace is true happiness.
3. Courage in difficult times is possible with the grace of God.
4. There are many examples of faith in the Gospels.
5. The words of Jesus bring joy and hope to the hearts of those who love Him.
6. To instruct children in the knowledge of the laws of God is an important duty of parents.
7. Anger is conquered by love as evil is conquered by good.
8. In marriage, a man and a woman promise to love each other in sickness and in health.
9. St. Elizabeth Ann Seton recognized the truthfulness of the Catholic Faith.
10. His perseverance was recognized by the general.

NOUNS

Lesson 4

Qualities of Nouns: Person

> There are four qualities of nouns: person, number, gender, and case.
>
> **Person** is the quality of a noun that indicates whether the noun is the **first person** (speaker), the **second person** (one spoken to), or the **third person** (one spoken about).

I, the **teacher**, said, "**Children**, please take out your history **book**."

In this sentence, the noun **teacher** is in the **first person** because it refers to the speaker.
The noun **children** is in the **second person** because it refers to the ones spoken to.
The noun **book** is in the **third person** because it refers to the one spoken about.

We **children** pray for the poor **souls** in **Purgatory**.

In this sentence, the noun **children** is in the **first person** because it refers to the speaker.
The nouns **souls** and **Purgatory** are in the third person because they refer to the ones spoken about.

Exercise 4: For the following sentences, please write on the lines the number for the person of each noun printed in italics.

1. The *pope* in Rome is the head of the Catholic Church. _____

2. We Seton *students* benefit from a solid Catholic *education*. _____ _____

3. St. Jude, *patron* of impossible *cases*, pray for us *sinners*. _____ _____ _____

4. I, your befuddled *son*, am asking, "Can you help me with my *homework*, *Dad*?" _____ _____ _____

5. *Children*, listen to your *parents*. _____ _____

6. The angel said, "Arise, *Joseph*, take the Child and His *mother* and flee into *Egypt*. _____ _____ _____

7. I, your *Lord*, say to you, let the *children* come. _____ _____

8. *Fr. Delaney*, were you the *pastor* when you lived in Connecticut? _____ _____

9. Holy Mary, *Mother* of *God*, pray for us *sinners*. _____ _____ _____

10. *Parents*, I am *Sister Margaret*, and I will speak to you about the new *course*. _____ _____ _____

Saint Thomas More, Pray for us!

Lesson 5: NOUNS

Qualities of Nouns: Number

> There are four qualities of nouns: person, number, gender, and case.
>
> **Number** is the quality of a noun that indicates whether the noun is **singular** (names one person, place, or thing) or **plural** (names two or more persons, places, or things).

Rules for Forming the Plural of Nouns

1. Most nouns form the plural by adding *s*.

2. Nouns ending in *s, x, z, ch,* and *sh* form the plural by adding *es*.

circus	mass	hoax	buzz	crutch	parish
circuses	masses	hoaxes	buzzes	crutches	parishes

3a. Nouns ending in *y* preceded by a consonant form the plural by changing the *y* to *i* and adding *es*.

mystery	monastery	ferry	heresy	variety	century
mysteries	monasteries	ferries	heresies	varieties	centuries

3b. Nouns ending in *y* preceded by a vowel form the plural by adding *s* to the singular.

play	Sunday	turkey	toy	buoy	guy
plays	Sundays	turkeys	toys	buoys	guys

4a. Most nouns ending in *f* or *fe* form the plural by adding *s*.

motif	staff	cliff	safe	giraffe	handkerchief
motifs	staffs	cliffs	safes	giraffes	handkerchiefs

4b. Some nouns ending in *f* or *fe* form the plural by changing the *f* or *fe* to *ves*.

half	shelf	thief	life	wife	knife
halves	shelves	thieves	lives	wives	knives

5a. Nouns ending in *o* preceded by a vowel form the plural by adding *s*.

video	cameo	patio	studio	cuckoo	taboo
videos	cameos	patios	studios	cuckoos	taboos

5b. Some nouns ending in *o* preceded by a consonant form the plural by adding *es*.

potato	echo	hero	cargo	embargo	torpedo
potatoes	echoes	heroes	cargoes	embargoes	torpedoes

5c. Some nouns ending in *o* preceded by a consonant form the plural by adding *s*.

fiasco	memo	kimono	crescendo	piano	solo
fiascos	memos	kimonos	crescendos	pianos	solos

NOUNS

Lesson 5

5d. Some nouns ending in *o* **preceded by a consonant** form the plural by adding either *s* or *es*.

halo	motto	grotto	buffalo	lasso	domino
halos	mottos	grottos	buffalos	lassos	dominos
haloes	mottoes	grottoes	buffaloes	lassoes	dominoes

Nouns ending in *o* **preceded by a consonant** are very tricky.
As with all words, when in doubt, refer to a dictionary.

6. Some nouns form the plural **by a change within the singular**.

man	woman	mouse	goose	foot	tooth
men	women	mice	geese	feet	teeth

7. A few nouns form the plural by **changing the ending to *en***.

ox   child
oxen   children

8. Some nouns have the **same form in the plural as in the singular**.

corps	Portuguese	deer	salmon	sheep	trout
corps	Portuguese	deer	salmon	sheep	trout

9a. Compound nouns usually form the plural by adding *s* to the principal word.

sister-in law	passer-by	teeter-totter	cross-stitch
sisters-in-law	passers-by	teeter-totters	cross-stitches

9b. Compound nouns ending in *ful* form the plural by adding *s*.

cupful	glassful	teaspoonful	bucketful	handful	bowlful
cupfuls	glassfuls	teaspoonfuls	bucketfuls	handfuls	bowlfuls

10. Some nouns are **used only in the plural**.

goods   tongs   scissors   trousers   tweezers   shears

11. Some nouns are **plural in form but singular in meaning**.

economics   news   measles   molasses   mumps   mathematics

12a. Letters, numbers, and symbols form the plural by adding *s*.

DVD	ABC	100	1940	$	%
DVDs	ABCs	100s	1940s	$s	%s

12b. Letters that would be confusing if *s* alone were added form the plural by adding *'s*.

I	A	U	i	a	u
I's	A's	U's	i's	a's	u's

13. When a name is preceded by a title, either the name or the title may be pluralized.
Since *Mrs.* cannot be pluralized, the surname must always be the part pluralized.

Dr. Smith	Mrs. Taylor	Reverend Mason	Father Wyatt
The Drs. Smith	The Mrs. Taylors	The Reverends Mason	The Fathers Wyatt
The Dr. Smiths		The Reverend Masons	The Father Wyatts

Lesson 5: NOUNS

Exercise 5A: For the following nouns, please write the plural if the noun is singular and the singular if it is plural.

1. radio _____
2. herd _____
3. sheep _____
4. X _____
5. 1960 _____
6. colony _____
7. flamingo _____
8. mice _____
9. tomatoes _____
10. leaf _____
11. Mrs. Grant _____
12. crucifixes _____
13. Tuesday _____
14. chief _____
15. sister-in-law _____
16. geese _____
17. moose _____
18. mathematics _____
19. lieutenant _____
20. Chinese _____

Exercise 5B: Write the plural form of the following nouns:

1. blessing _____
2. onyx _____
3. Mass _____
4. mouthful _____
5. trout _____
6. donkey _____
7. 1000 _____
8. dozen _____
9. half _____
10. staff _____
11. icon _____
12. attorney general _____
13. woman _____
14. lady _____
15. patio _____
16. jigsaw _____
17. corpse _____
18. crop _____
19. corps _____
20. kimono _____

NOUNS

Lesson 6

Qualities of Nouns: Gender

> There are four qualities of nouns: person, number, gender, and case.
>
> **Gender** is the **quality** of a noun that indicates whether the noun is **masculine**, **feminine**, or **neuter**.
> A noun that indicates **male** is **masculine** in gender.
> A noun that may indicate **either masculine or feminine** is considered **masculine** in gender.
> A noun that indicates **female** is **feminine** in gender.
> A noun that indicates **neither male nor female** is **neuter** in gender.

Male	Male	Female	Neuter
priest	attorney	nun	vocation
landlord	owner	landlady	property
prince	ruler	queen	kingdom
bachelor	firefighter	actress	profession
abbot	mayor	niece	career
stallion	sheep	mare	farm

Exercise 6: In the space provided for each of the following nouns, indicate the gender by writing M (masculine), F (feminine), or N (neuter).

1. mother _____
2. uncle _____
3. democracy _____
4. senator _____
5. lord _____
6. hostess _____
7. Martha _____
8. church _____
9. creativity _____
10. emperor _____
11. scapular _____
12. cow _____
13. doctor _____
14. wife _____
15. relic _____
16. Jerusalem _____
17. theology _____
18. theologian _____
19. spinster _____
20. kangaroo _____
21. classmate _____
22. table _____
23. Herod _____
24. pilot _____
25. child _____
26. insomnia _____
27. shepherd _____
28. guest _____
29. saint _____
30. waitress _____

Lesson 6

NOUNS

Qualities of Nouns: Case

There are four qualities of nouns: person, number, gender, and case.

Each noun in a sentence performs a specific **function**.
Case is the **quality** of a noun that indicates the **function** of that noun in a sentence.
The three cases of nouns are **nominative**, **possessive**, and **objective**.

Nominative Case

Nominative Case: A noun that functions as a **subject**, a **subjective complement**, a **direct address** or an **exclamation** in a sentence is in the **nominative case**.

An **appositive** that explains a subject, a subjective complement, or a direct address is in the **nominative case**.

Possessive Case

Possessive Case: The function of a noun in the possessive case in a sentence is to **show possession** or **ownership**.

Objective Case

Objective Case: A noun that functions as a **direct object**, an **indirect object**, or an **object of a preposition** in a sentence is in the **objective case**.

An **appositive** that explains a direct object, an indirect object, or an object of a preposition is in the **objective case**.

NOUNS

Lesson 6

Diagrams help us to visualize the function of nouns in a sentence.

1. Kristen, Charles gave Danny, your cousin, the book with St. George's picture.

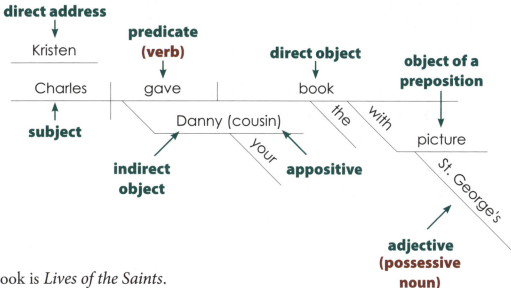

2. The book is *Lives of the Saints*.

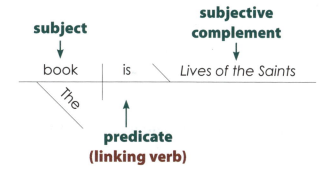

3. After prayerful deliberation, the pope selected Joan of Arc leader of the French troops.

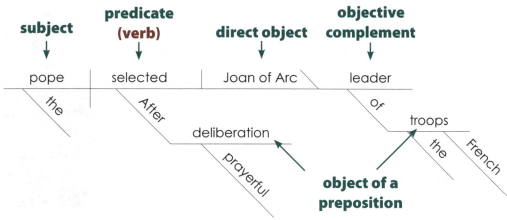

Lesson 7: NOUNS

Nominative Case: Subject

> A noun that functions as a **subject** in a sentence is in the nominative case.
> The **subject** answers the question *who?* or *what?* before the verb.
> A verb is the part of speech that expresses action, being, or state of being.

The **pope** invigorated Cuba by his visit.

Priests and **nuns** spread the Gospel to the people.

Cuba is a communist country.

There are several nouns in these sentences. The nouns in bold are subjects because they answer the questions *who?* or *what?* before the verb. One sentence has two nouns that function as subjects.

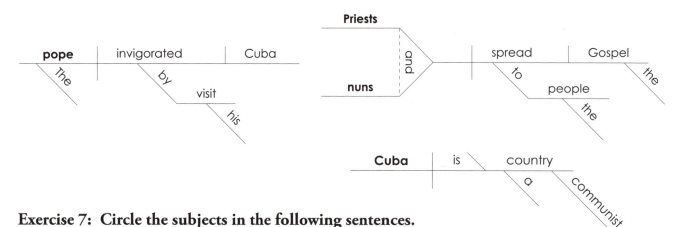

Exercise 7: Circle the subjects in the following sentences.

1. The martyrs loved Jesus very much.
2. St. Peter denied Jesus three times.
3. Jesus came to save us all.
4. The Scribes and Pharisees looked for a way to put Jesus to death.
5. A poor widow cast two pennies into the church collection.
6. As a result of their lack of faith, the apostles were afraid in the storm.
7. Jesus addressed the young man directly.
8. News of the miracle spread throughout the land.
9. Monica, will you and David attend the prayer service?
10. The senior class went on a field trip to the Shrine of the Immaculate Conception.

NOUNS

Lesson 8

Nominative Case: Subjective Complement

A noun that functions as a **subjective complement** in a sentence is in the nominative case.

A noun that functions as a subjective complement **follows a linking verb**.

A subjective complement **refers to the subject**.

A **linking verb** expresses *being*, and it is any form of the verb *be*:
am, is, are, was, were, be, been, being.

Some verbs are linking verbs when they express *state of being*, and they may be replaced by a form of the verb *be*:
become, seem, remain, feel, taste, smell, appear, look, grow, sound.

The pope is the **leader** of the Catholic Church.
Karol Wojtyla was a Polish **cardinal**.
The cardinal became **pope** in 1978.
The pope's name was **John Paul II**.
This leader of millions remained a humble **man**.

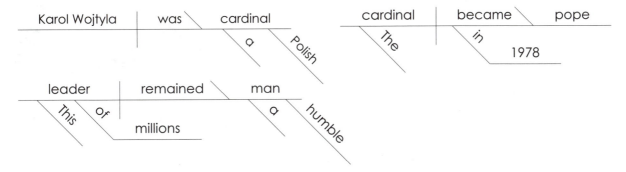

Exercise 8: Circle the subjective complements in the following sentences.

1. Every soul is a traveler on his way to heaven.
2. Prudence is the virtue that disposes practical reason to discern our true good.
3. St. Paul became a strong leader in spreading Christianity among the Gentiles.
4. Jesus is Immanuel; He is "God-is-with-us."
5. Our Lord forever remains our Savior.
6. Mortal sin is sin whose object is grave matter.

Lesson 9

NOUNS

Nominative Case: Direct Address

A noun that functions as a **direct address** in a sentence is in the nominative case.
A **direct address** is the person, place, or thing spoken to and named.
A direct address is separated from other words in a sentence by commas.

Kristin, could you bring me that book?
The answer, **Mark**, is five.
Obey your parents, **children**.

```
Kristin
────────
you │ could bring │ book
    │         \me │ \that

Mark
────────
      answer │ is \ five
         \The

children
────────
(you) │ Obey │ parents
              \your
```

Exercise 9: Circle the direct address in the following sentences.

1. While I sleep, Mary, offer Jesus the beatings of my heart as fervent acts of love.

2. Into your hands, Lord, I commend my spirit.

3. Here I am, Lord.

4. Joseph, take the Child and His mother and flee into Egypt.

5. Teacher, what must I do to inherit everlasting life?

6. You have been blessed by the presence of the Holy One, Jerusalem.

7. Matthew, Mark, Luke, and John, Carol, are the four evangelists.

8. Death, where is thy sting?

NOUNS

Lesson 10

Nominative Case: Appositive

> An **appositive** follows another noun or a pronoun to identify or explain that noun or pronoun.
> A noun that functions as an **appositive** in a sentence is in the nominative case when it explains the subject, the subjective complement, or a direct address.
> There is no verb between the appositive and the noun it explains.
> There is usually a comma before and after the appositive and its modifiers.

Elizabeth Ann Seton, **founder** of the Sisters of Charity, began her apostolate in 1809.
The young French girl in uniform was their leader, **Joan of Arc**.
Jacob, my **son**, have you sold your birthright?

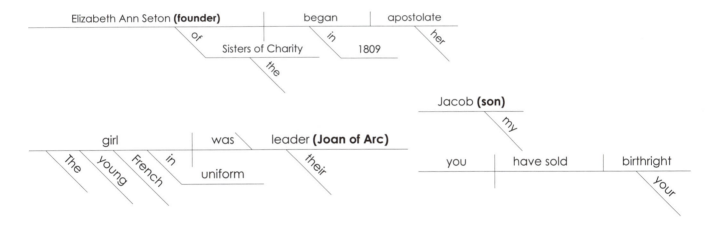

Exercise 10: Underline all the nouns in the following sentences. Circle the nouns used as appositives.

1. Fortitude, a moral virtue, ensures firmness in difficulties and constancy in the pursuit of good.

2. Pope St. Leo, a Doctor of the Church, persuaded Attila to leave Rome untouched.

3. Columbus' three ships, the *Nina*, the *Pinta*, and the *Santa Maria*, sailed toward the East Indies.

4. Dominic Savio, a student of St. John Bosco, was a teenager when he died.

5. The founder of the sodality is Fr. Jones, our pastor.

6. Mesopotamia, land of kings, you have been blessed with prosperity.

7. John Paul II, the pontiff, called for social justice and religious freedom in the world.

Lesson 11: NOUNS

Nominative Case: Exclamation

A noun that functions as an **exclamation** in a sentence is in the nominative case. An **exclamation** is a noun that is used independently in a sentence to express a strong emotion.

Drinks! We forgot the drinks!
His **letter!** I did not mail it!
The **novena!** It begins tonight at the church.

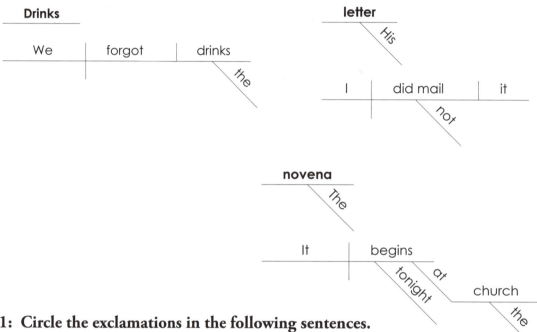

Exercise 11: Circle the exclamations in the following sentences.

1. Christopher! He is the first one here!
2. Guardian Angel! How he loves to protect me!
3. Poor souls! We must pray for those in Purgatory!
4. Straight and narrow path! It is my way to Heaven!
5. Dirty clothes pile! Won't it ever disappear!

NOUNS

Lesson 12

Nominative Case Review

Exercise 12A: In the following sentences, circle all the nouns which are in the nominative case. Above each noun, indicate its function by writing S for subject, SC for subjective complement, AP for appositive, DA for direct address, or E for exclamation.

1. Baptism is a sacrament which gives the soul an indelible spiritual mark.

2. Confirmation, a sacrament, gives us the seven gifts of the Holy Spirit.

3. Confession! That is just what I need!

4. O my God, I am heartily sorry for having offended Thee.

5. The apostles, the first priests and bishops, were the first men to receive the Body and Blood of Christ.

6. On Easter Sunday night, Jesus gave His apostles the power to forgive sins in His name.

7. The apostles passed their priestly power on to other men through Holy Orders.

8. Mary, my mother, despise not my petitions, but, in your mercy, hear and answer me.

9. Jesus in the Blessed Sacrament loves little children.

10. Simon Peter was a fisherman from Galilee.

Exercise 12B: Diagram the following sentences:

1. Peter, you are rock.

2. Jesus, our Savior, loves us.

Lesson 13: NOUNS

Possessive Case: Rules for Forming

A **noun** whose function is to show **possession or ownership** is in the **possessive case**. Because of their function, such nouns are used as adjectives (words that modify a noun). Nouns in the possessive case may be singular or plural.

Jane's gloves are green.   The **boys'** bikes were decorated for the parade.

Add **'s** to form the possessive of a singular noun (including singular and plural compound nouns).

Common Noun	Possessive	Compound Noun	Possessive	Proper Noun	Possessive*
saint	saint's	editor-in-chief	editor-in-chief's	Sunday	Sunday's
church	church's	daughters-in-law	daughters-in-law's	James	James'
godmother	godmother's	attorney general	attorney general's	Jesus	Jesus'
writer	writer's	maid of honor	maid of honor's	Moses	Moses'

*For possessive nouns ending in *s*, some grammarians accept *'s* (e.g. James's).

Add **'s** to form the possessive of a plural noun that does not end in **s**.

Noun	Possessive
oxen	oxen's
mice	mice's
deer	deer's
women	women's

Add **only an apostrophe** to form the possessive of a plural noun that ends in **s**.

Noun	Possessive	Noun	Possessive
saints	saints'	Aprils	Aprils'
churches	churches'	Clarks	Clarks'
godmothers	godmothers'	Joneses	Joneses'

NOUNS

Lesson 13

Exercise 13A: Write the singular possessive and the plural possessive of each noun.

Noun	Singular Possessive	Plural Possessive
1. priest		
2. fox		
3. baby		
4. sister-in-law		
5. altar boy		
6. city		
7. mouse		
8. pope		
9. gentleman		
10. Catholic		
11. moose		
12. patio		
13. chair		
14. queen		
15. wife		
16. child		
17. Mrs. Finch		
18. turkey		
19. potato		
20. cliff		

Saint Thomas More, Pray for us! J.M.J.

Lesson 13: NOUNS

Possessive Case: Separate and Joint Possession

Separate Possession — Sometimes two or more nouns are used together to show that each one owns or possesses something independently. In this case, after each noun, add *'s* (for a singular noun or a plural noun that does not end in *s*) or an *'* **only** (for a plural noun that ends in *s*).

Joint Possession — Sometimes two or more nouns are used together to show that all own or possess something together or as a group. In this case, after the last noun only, add *'s* (for a singular noun or a plural noun that does not end in *s*) or an *'* **only** (for a plural noun that ends in *s*).

St. Luke's and St. John's Gospels are the last two in the Bible.
  (St. Luke and St. John possess a gospel each.)

The **cardinals' and the bishops'** residences prominently display a portrait of the pope.
  (The cardinals and the bishops own residences independently of each other.)

Mary and Sally's mother made the birthday cake.
  (Mary and Sally possess one mother together.)

The **athletes and soldiers'** patron is St. Sebastian.
  (Athletes and soldiers possess one patron saint together.)

Exercise 13B: Fill in the blanks with the possessive form of the nouns given for each sentence.

Martha, Mary   1. _____ and _____ brother was raised from the dead.

Judas, Peter   2. _____ and _____ denials of Christ ended in very different ways.

boys, girls   3. The _____ and _____ preparation for the sacraments was made by their parents.

brother, sister   4. Did you put away your _____ and _____ clothes?

Paula, Rose   5. _____ and _____ papers came in second and third place.

Anthony, Paul   6. _____ and _____ baptisms were on the same day.

directors, singers 7. Choir _____ and _____ patron is St. Gregory the Great.

Adam, Eve   8. _____ and _____ fall into temptation caused all of us to be born with original sin.

NOUNS

Lesson 14

Objective Case: Direct Object

> **Objective Case:** A noun that functions as a **direct object**, an **indirect object**, an **object of a preposition,** or an **objective complement** in a sentence is in the **objective case**.
>
> An **appositive** that explains a direct object, an indirect object, an object of a preposition, or an objective complement is in the **objective case**.

> A noun that functions as a **direct object** in a sentence is in the **objective case**. The **direct object** answers the question *whom?* or *what?* after the verb.

Christopher Columbus discovered **America**. (discovered *what?*)
We crown **Mary**, our mother in Heaven. (crown *whom?*)
The congregation released a **movie** about the life of Christ. (released *what?*)

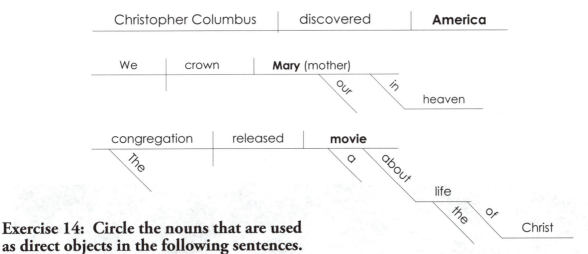

Exercise 14: Circle the nouns that are used as direct objects in the following sentences.

1. Be patient and swallow your resentment.

2. Destroy this Temple and in three days I will rebuild it.

3. Peter denied Jesus in the courtyard.

4. We must prepare a way for the Lord.

5. Pope John Paul II visited Cuba in January of 1998.

Saint Thomas More, Pray for us!   J.M.J.   English 8 for Young Catholics

Lesson 15: NOUNS

Objective Case: Cognate Object

A noun that functions as a **cognate object** in a sentence is in the **objective case**. A **cognate object** is a direct object that repeats the meaning of the verb and closely resembles it.

The Church will always teach the **teachings** of Jesus.
We shall dance a **dance** of joy when abortions are stopped.
I hope to die the **death** of a just man.

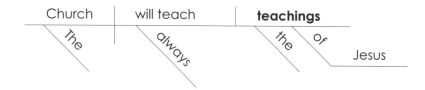

Exercise 15A: Circle the nouns used as cognate objects in the following sentences.

1. In the time of Noah, it rained more rain than the earth had ever seen.
2. We mailed the mail directly from the post office.
3. Michael and Theresa both rode the waterfall ride.
4. I drew this drawing to reflect the face of Jesus from the Shroud.
5. Anytime someone arrives late, he says the same old saying.

NOUNS

Lesson 15

Objective Case: Objective Complement

> A noun that functions as an **objective complement** in a sentence is in the **objective case**. An **objective complement** is a second object, and it explains the meaning of the direct object.

The boss appointed Michael **secretary**.
The angel Gabriel named Mary's Child **Jesus**.
My parents chose Laura **baby-sitter**.

Exercise 15B: Circle the nouns used as objective complements in the following sentences.

1. The disciples chose Stephen deacon.
2. The young pro-lifers named their club "Holy Innocents."
3. St. John Bosco called the old barn "The Oratory."
4. We are electing Paul treasurer.
5. Pope John Paul II appointed Bishop Francis George cardinal.

Lesson 16: NOUNS

Objective Case: Adverbial Objective

> A noun that functions as an **adverbial objective** in a sentence is in the **objective case**. An **adverbial objective** is a noun that is used as an adverb. Such nouns may tell *when, where, how long, how high, how far,* or *how much*.

We go to Mass every **day**. (tells *when*)
The church is twenty **minutes** from our house. (tells *how long*)
The ball bounced ten **feet** into the air. (tells *how high*)

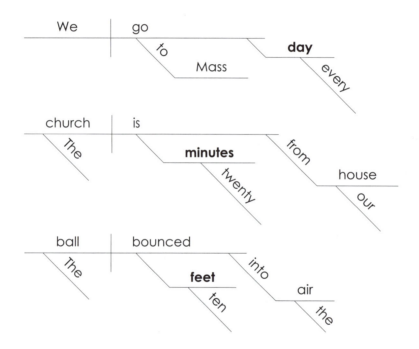

Exercise 16: Circle the nouns used as adverbial objectives in the following sentences.

1. The cardinals traveled three days.
2. May you be in heaven a half-hour before the devil knows you are dead!
3. We arrived forty minutes early.
4. Stuart ran twelve miles in last Sunday's race.
5. Our tree house sits six feet off the ground.

NOUNS

Lesson 17

Objective Case: Indirect Object

> A noun that functions as an **indirect object** in a sentence is in the **objective case**. The **indirect object** answers the questions *to whom? for whom?* or *to what?* after the verb.
> An indirect object is always followed by a direct object.

> The words *to* and *for* are not used with an indirect object. *To* and *for* are prepositions and the words that follow them are objects of a preposition.

Jesus granted the **apostles** power over demons. (granted *to whom?*)
Grandpa buys **Grandma** flowers for her birthday. (buys *for whom?*)
Roger gives the **plant** a little water every day. (give *to what?*)

Exercise 17: Circle the nouns that are used as indirect objects in each sentence.

1. The devil offered Jesus the kingdoms of the world.
2. God sent Mary an angel to ask her to be the mother of Jesus.
3. They presented Mother Teresa the Nobel Peace Prize.
4. Fr. Damien gave the lepers of Molokai a church and attended to their spiritual needs.
5. I gave the seminary a donation.
6. Father teaches the children the sacraments, and he teaches the commandments as well.
7. Mr. Sawyer built the children a new gym set for Christmas.
8. Mail your aunt a thank-you note.
9. Claire, give your sister a bib for the baby.

Saint Thomas More, Pray for us!   J.M.J.   English 8 for Young Catholics

Lesson 18: NOUNS

Objective Case: Object of a Preposition

> A noun that functions as an **object of a preposition** in a sentence is in the **objective case**. An **object of a preposition** follows a preposition.

Commonly Used Prepositions

about	around	by	in	through
above	at	down	near	to
across	before	during	of	toward
after	behind	except	off	under
against	beside	for	on	up
among	between	from	over	with

Damien worked *among* the **lepers** on the **island** of **Molokai**.
He eventually died *from* the **disease** himself.
He had followed faithfully *in* Christ's **footsteps**.

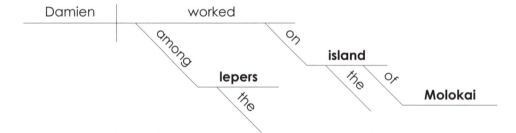

Exercise 18: Circle all the nouns that are the objects of a preposition in each sentence.

1. In Boston, Our Lady's shrine is a worthwhile detour for visitors to the city.
2. In the shrine, there is an icon in a golden frame which is ornate with rays.
3. Two "vases" filled with neatly arranged crutches and canes stand on either side of the altar.
4. They are reminders of the many cures granted at this shrine.
5. Visitors will find an abundance of other stops in historic Boston.
6. During the summer, tourists get off buses near Haymarket Square.
7. Hundreds make their way among the crowd toward Faneuil Hall, Boston's original house of legislature.
8. Many people conclude their tour with a visit to Old North Church.
9. Inside the church, they gaze up the stairs to the tower where Paul Revere waited for the British.
10. With souvenirs in their bags, they head home, grateful to God for his many blessings.

NOUNS

Lesson 19

Objective Case: Appositive

> An **appositive** follows another noun or pronoun to identify or explain that noun or pronoun. A noun that functions as an **appositive** in a sentence is in the objective case when it explains the direct object, objective complement, indirect object, or object of a preposition. There is usually a comma before and after the appositive and its modifiers.

We praise God, our heavenly **Father**. (appositive of the direct object)
The club appointed Matthew secretary, his usual **job**. (appositive of the objective complement)
They gave Agnes, the new **bride**, a set of towels. (appositive of the indirect object)
We invited Jim to St. Mary's, our **church**, for Mass. (appositive of the object of the preposition)

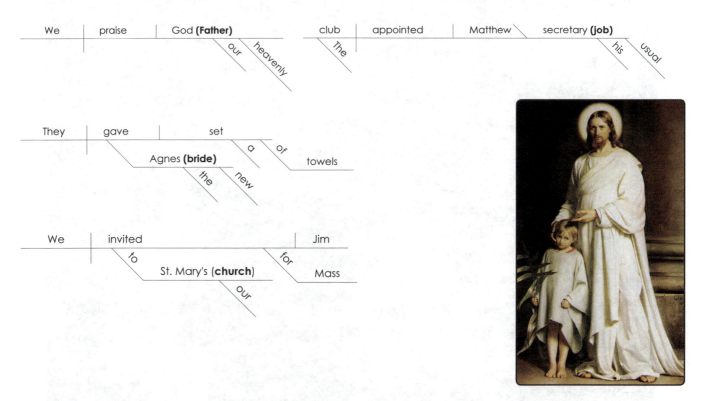

Exercise 19: Circle the appositive in the objective case in each sentence.

1. We are always in the presence of God, our Father, especially when we are in church.
2. Emperor Diocletian tortured St. George, a great martyr of the early Church.
3. King Herod killed St. John, the precursor of Jesus.
4. The committee selected Mother Teresa, a humble nun, recipient of the Nobel Peace Prize.
5. We give Seton, a home study program, thanks for a solid Catholic education.

NOUNS

CHAPTER 2

PRONOUNS

PRONOUNS

PRONOUNS

Chapter Outline

CHAPTER TWO

I. **Personal pronouns**
   A. Person, number, and gender
   B. Nominative case: *I, you, he, she, it, we, they*
   C. Objective case: *me, you, him, her, it, us, them*
   D. Use with *than* and *as*
   E. Compound personal pronouns (reflexive and intensive):
      myself, yourself, himself, herself, itself, ourselves, yourselves, themselves
   F. Possessive pronouns:
      mine, yours, his, hers, ours, yours, theirs

II. **Demonstrative pronouns**
   this, that, these, those

III. **Interrogative pronouns**
   who, whom, which, whose, what

IV. **Relative pronouns**
   who, whom, that, whose, which

V. **Indefinite pronouns**
   A. Always singular
      another, each, either, neither,
      much, one, other,
      anybody, everybody, nobody, somebody,
      anyone, everyone, no one, someone,
      anything, everything, nothing, something
   B. Always plural
      both, few, many, most, several, others
   C. Singular or plural
      all, any, enough, more,
      none, same, some, such

Lesson 20: PRONOUNS

Diagrams help us to visualize the function of pronouns in a sentence.

1. They and Sandra gave her one for Christmas, and Frank bought himself his with them.

   (personal, personal, personal [indefinite], personal, personal [possessive])

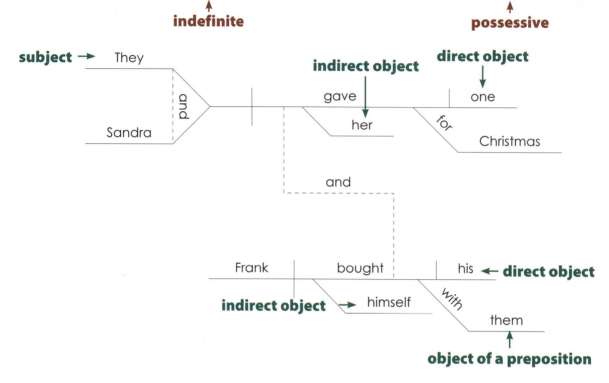

2. Who were they who chose that for him?

   (interrogative, personal, relative, personal [demonstrative])

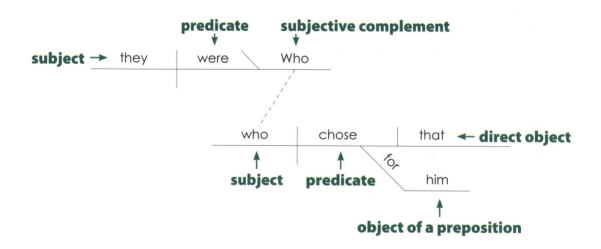

PRONOUNS

Lesson 20

Personal Pronouns

A **pronoun** is the part of speech that replaces a noun.
The noun to which the pronoun refers is its **antecedent**.
Kinds of pronouns: personal, demonstrative, interrogative, relative, and indefinite.

Pronouns have the same qualities as nouns: person, number, gender, and case.
In a sentence, a pronoun is in the **same person, number, and gender as its antecedent** (the noun to which it refers).
A pronoun's **case depends upon its function in the sentence.**

A **personal pronoun** refers to 1) the *speaker*, 2) the person, place, or thing *spoken to*, or 3) the person, place, or thing *spoken about*.

	SINGULAR	PLURAL
First Person (speaker)	I mine me	we ours us
Second Person (one spoken to)	you yours you	you yours you
Third Person (one spoken about)	he, she, it his, hers, its him, her, it	they theirs them

CASE	SINGULAR	PLURAL	FUNCTION IN SENTENCE
Nominative	I, you, he, she, it	we, you, they	subject, subjective complement
Objective	me, you, him, her, it	us, you, them	direct object, indirect object, object of a preposition
Nominative or Objective	mine, yours his, hers	ours, yours theirs	These are possessive pronouns, and they may be used for any function in a sentence.

Saint Thomas More, Pray for us!   J.M.J.   English 8 for Young Catholics

Lesson 20: PRONOUNS

Personal Pronouns: Person, Number, and Gender

The **crowds** cheered when they saw the **pope** approach.
He blessed **them** as **he** passed by.

The pronoun **he** is in the third person, singular, masculine (like its antecedent pope).
The pronoun **them** is in the third person, plural, masculine (like its antecedent crowds).

Exercise 20: Circle the personal pronouns in the following sentences and give the person, the number, and the gender of each.

Example: John the Baptist baptized people and preached to (them) in the desert.
_____3rd person, plural, masculine_____

1. The Holy Spirit loves us; He will preserve the Church from error.

2. "Turn away from sin and be baptized," he told the people, "and God will forgive you."

3. The One Who will come after me is much greater than I am.

4. John said, "I baptize you with water, but He will baptize you with the Holy Spirit."

5. Hail, Mary, full of grace! The Lord is with you.

6. You shall conceive and bear a Son and give Him the name Jesus.

7. He made His life ours.

8. He was conceived by the Holy Spirit within her.

9. Jesus said, "As the Father has sent Me, so I send you."

10. Then He breathed on them and said, "Receive the Holy Spirit."

PRONOUNS

Lesson 21

Personal Pronouns: Case: Nominative Case

Each **pronoun** in a sentence performs a specific **function**.
The **function** a **pronoun** performs in a sentence tells us the pronoun's **case**.
Pronouns may be in the **nominative case** or the **objective case**.

A pronoun that functions as a **subject** or a **subjective complement** in a sentence is in the **nominative case**.

The **subject** answers *who?* or *what?* before the verb.

The **subjective complement** follows a linking verb and refers to the subject. (A linking verb is any form of the verb *be*: *am, is, are, was, were*.)

Nominative Case Pronouns
I, you, he, she, it, we, they

Charles and **I** bought rosaries.

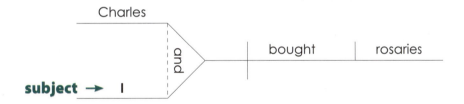

The man in the chapel is **he**.

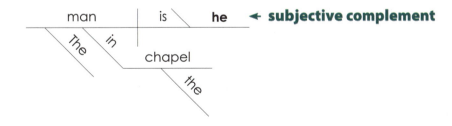

(subject)	Did **you** see the Smith twins among the crowd?
(subject)	**They** arrived earlier with Sarah.
(subjective complement)	The twins' godparents are Charles and **she**.
(subjective complement)	The last to arrive were **they**.

Saint Thomas More, Pray for us!   J.M.J.   English 8 for Young Catholics   37

Lesson 21: PRONOUNS

Exercise 21A: Circle the correct personal pronoun in each sentence.

1. (Them, **They**) and (me, **I**) are planning a trip to Italy.
2. Paul and (**we**, us) would like a window seat.
3. Catherine and (**she**, her) are looking forward to seeing the pope.
4. Every time (**we**, us) saw someone in white, (**they**, them) thought it might be (him, **he**).
5. Was it (him, **he**) who threw the coin in the Trevi Fountain?
6. (**They**, Them) and (**we**, us) visited the Colosseum.
7. It was (us, **we**) who prayed for the many martyrs.
8. Paul and (them, **they**) were the first to see St. Peter's, the largest church in all of Christendom.
9. (**They**, them) showed us the places on the floor of St. Peter's which mark the sizes of other churches.
10. (**We**, us) went down the stairs to see the tombs of the popes.
11. The Swiss Guards are (**they**, them) who guard the entrances to private passages of the Vatican.
12. It was (**he**, him) who caused the guard to salute.
13. (**We**, us) were able to attend an audience with the pope.
14. It was (me, **I**) who was able to kiss his hand.
15. The Vicar of Christ is (**he**, him).

Exercise 21B: Diagram the following sentences.

1. Jennifer and he prayed the Rosary.

2. The first participant was I.

PRONOUNS

Lesson 22

Personal Pronouns: Case: Objective Case

> The **function** a **pronoun** performs in a sentence tells us the pronoun's **case**. Pronouns may be in the **nominative case** or the **objective case**.

> A pronoun that functions as a **direct object**, an **indirect object**, or an **object of a preposition** is in the **objective case**.
>
> The **direct object** answers *whom?* or *what?* after the verb.
> The **indirect object** answers the question *to whom? for whom?* or *to what?* after the verb.
> The **object of a preposition** follows a preposition.

Objective Case Pronouns
me, you, him, her, it, us, them

Claire reads **him** a saint's story daily, and he tells **it** to **them** afterward.

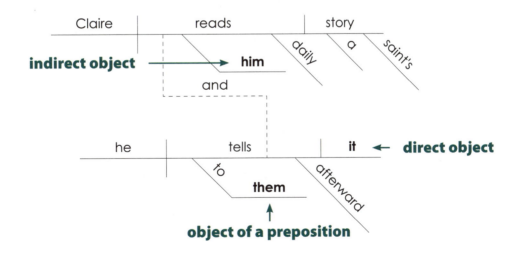

(direct object)	Margaret will see **him** next Sunday.
(indirect object)	Lord, show **us** the way.
(object of a preposition)	Go outside and play ball with your dad and **them**.

Saint Thomas More, Pray for us! — J.M.J. — English 8 for Young Catholics

Lesson 22: PRONOUNS

Exercise 22: Circle the correct personal pronoun(s) in each sentence. Above each pronoun, write DO (direct object), IO (indirect object), or OP (object of a preposition) to indicate its function in the sentence.

1. God loves (we, **us**) all, even to the point of dying on the Cross for (we, **us**).

2. The Son of God teaches (we, **us**) through the Catholic Church.

3. An angel appeared to the shepherds and brought (they, **them**) good tidings of great joy.

4. God is in Heaven. All good children will go to (He, **Him**).

5. At an early age, Susan's mother gave (she, **her**) swimming lessons.

6. We did not see (he, **him**) at the tennis court.

7. All who met (she, **her**) liked (she, **her**).

8. How many good friends God has given (we, **us**)!

9. Their love means so much to (I, **me**).

10. We must help (they, **them**) when they are sick.

11. If you want to be a disciple of Mine, you must take up your cross every day and follow (I, **Me**).

12. Elizabeth Seton prayed that God would give (she, **her**) the light to walk in the way that leads to (He, **Him**).

13. She asked, (**He**, Him) to give her faith, hope, and love."

14. Many of her family and friends rejected (she, **her**) because she became a Catholic.

15. In 1809, Elizabeth took religious vows. Several other women joined (she, **her**).

16. Elizabeth told (they, **them**): "In our daily work we must do the will of God."

17. She considered her conversion to Catholicism as God's greatest grace to (she, **her**).

18. The first American parochial school was begun by (she, **her**).

19. God has given (I, **me**) a great deal to do; may I always choose His will over my own.

20. Soul of Christ, make (I, **me**) holy; Blood of Christ, wash (I, **me**) clean of my sins.

PRONOUNS

Lesson 23

Personal Pronouns: Use with *Than* and *As*

> A conjunction is the part of speech that connects words, phrases, or clauses in a sentence. The **conjunctions** *than* and *as* in a sentence are used for comparison.
>
> The personal pronoun that follows the conjunction *than* or *as* must be in the same case as the word with which it is compared.

> A complete sentence that includes the **conjunction** *than* or *as* followed by a **personal pronoun** omits some words from the sentence.
>
> Choose the case (nominative or objective) of the pronoun that you would use if the missing words were present.

                    subject ↓   **indirect objects** ↓ ↓

Betty knows Max better than **Mildred** knows him.   Mom gave me as much as she gave **Bob** and **Bill**.
Betty knows Max better than **she**.   Mom gave me as much as she gave **them**.
    nominative case pronoun ↑   **objective case pronoun** ↑

                  direct object ↓   **subjects** ↓ ↓

Betty knows Max better than she knows **Sue**.   Mom gave me as much as **Bob** and **Bill** gave me.
Betty knows Max better than **her**.   Mom gave me as much as **they**.
    objective case pronoun ↑   **nominative case pronoun** ↑

                    subject ↓   **subject** ↓

Tim has played soccer longer than **Dan** has played.   Carey is as tall as **Jennifer** is tall.
Tim has played soccer longer than **he**.   Carey is as tall as **she**.
    nominative case pronoun ↑   **nominative case pronoun** ↑

Betty knows Max better than **she**.

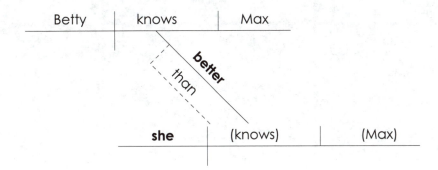

Saint Thomas More, Pray for us!   J.M.J.   English 8 for Young Catholics

Lesson 23

PRONOUNS

Exercise 23: Circle the correct pronoun in each sentence.

1. She sings better than (I, me) at church during Mass.
   [*Think: She sings better than (I, me) sing.*]

2. They arrived at church earlier than (we, us).
   [*Think: They arrived at church earlier than (we, us) arrived.*]

3. He has been to Rome more often than (she, her).

4. I will try as much as (they, them) to get to Heaven.

5. They strive to be as good as (he, him).

6. There is more jelly in here for me than (he, him).

7. We will be truly happy when we live our lives as (he, him).

8. Mother Teresa has performed more good works than (I, me).

9. Catherine has traveled to Rome more than (she, her).

10. We study as much as (they, them).

11. I have memorized the Baltimore Catechism as much as (she, her).

12. My brothers are older than (I, me).

13. They have more experience than (we, us).

14. In the seminary, St. John Vianney was slower than (they, them).

15. Nonetheless, he studied more diligently than (they, them).

PRONOUNS

Lesson 24

Compound Personal Pronouns

A **compound personal pronoun** is formed by adding **self** (singular) or **selves** (plural) to certain forms of personal pronouns.

Compound Personal Pronouns

	SINGULAR	PLURAL
First Person	*myself*	*ourselves*
Second Person	*yourself*	*yourselves*
Third Person	*himself, herself, itself*	*themselves*

A **reflexive compound personal pronoun**
- follows the verb in a sentence,
- refers back to the subject,
- may function as a direct object, an indirect object, or an object of a preposition,
- must agree with its antecedent (the noun to which it refers) in person, number, and gender, and
- is required to complete the meaning of the sentence.

An **intensive compound personal pronoun**
- is often found immediately after the noun or pronoun it emphasizes,
- is used to emphasize a preceding noun or pronoun, and
- is not required to complete the meaning of the sentence.

Reflexive	God gave **Himself** to us on the Cross.
Intensive	He **Himself** died on the Cross.
Reflexive	I bought **myself** a dress.
Intensive	I **myself** bought a dress.
Reflexive	You go to Confession by **yourselves**.
Intensive	You **yourselves** go to Confession.

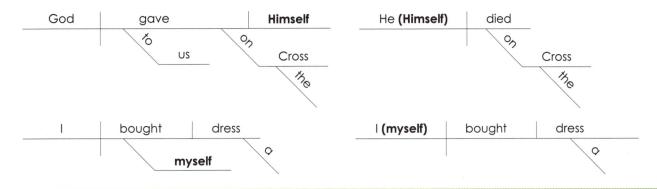

Saint Thomas More, Pray for us!   J.M.J.   English 8 for Young Catholics

Lesson 24: PRONOUNS

Exercise 24A: Circle the compound personal pronouns in each sentence. On the lines to the right, write whether they are reflexive or intensive.

1. God *Himself* created the world out of love. _____
2. We *ourselves* should thank God daily for the gift of life. _____
3. We give *ourselves* back to Christ by doing His will. _____
4. He *Himself* asks this of us. _____
5. Sacrifice *itself* is useless without love. _____
6. We can sacrifice *ourselves* in many ways. _____
7. Mother Teresa offered *herself* to the poor and the sick. _____
8. The pope *himself* prays for the Church daily. _____
9. St. Peter *himself* died upside down upon a cross. _____
10. Our parents give *themselves* to us every day in many hidden ways. _____
11. As children, we *ourselves* should listen to our parents. _____
12. They seated *themselves* at the meeting. _____
13. They bought *themselves* rosaries at the Catholic Shop. _____
14. We purify *ourselves* through Confession. _____
15. In receiving Holy Communion, we are united to God *Himself*. _____

Exercise 24B: Diagram the following sentences.

1. We offer ourselves to God.

2. The children tell themselves stories.

3. You yourselves should lead the parade.

PRONOUNS

Lesson 25

Personal Pronouns: Possessive Pronouns

A **possessive personal pronoun** shows **possession** or **ownership**.
As with all personal pronouns, a possessive pronoun retains the same person, number, and gender as its antecedent (the noun to which it refers).
A possessive personal pronoun may be in the **nominative case or the objective case**, depending on its function in a sentence.
Possessive personal pronouns do not use apostrophes.

Possessive Personal Pronouns

	SINGULAR	PLURAL
First Person	mine	ours
Second Person	yours	yours
Third Person	his, hers, its*	theirs

The *pronoun *its* is not used in a sentence. Instead, to indicate the possessive of a neuter noun, use the possessive noun.
For example, the sentence *The shovel's broken handle had to be repaired* cannot be changed to *Its had to be repaired*.
If we change the sentence to read, *Its handle had to be repaired*, then we are using the <u>adjective</u> *its*.

Nominative Case

(subject)   **Mine** is the white rosary.

(subjective complement)   The blue rosary is **his**.

Objective Case

(direct object)   Rosemary lost **yours**.

(indirect object)   Fr. Davis gave **theirs** a blessing.

(object of a preposition)   Put your luggage with **ours**.

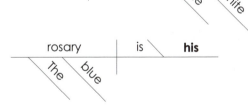

Saint Thomas More, Pray for us!   J.M.J.   English 8 for Young Catholics

Lesson 25: PRONOUNS

Exercise 25A: Circle the possessive pronoun in each sentence. On the lines to the right, write its function in the sentence.

1. Give ours your undivided attention. _____

2. Mine is to do the will of God. _____

3. If you forgive their failings, God will forgive yours. _____

4. Please hand me his. _____

5. Why do you see the splinter in your brother's eye and _____
   not notice the log in yours?

6. Blessed are the poor in spirit; the kingdom of Heaven is theirs. _____

7. I know where my treasure is. Where is yours? _____

8. He gives theirs an extra scoop of ice cream. _____

9. Ours is in the chapel. _____

10. You pray for our perseverance, and we pray for yours. _____

Exercise 25B: Diagram the following sentences.

1. Yours is the Kingdom.

2. Park your car behind ours.

3. He will pay his to her.

PRONOUNS

Lesson 26

Demonstrative Pronouns

A **demonstrative pronoun** points to a specific person, place, or thing. A **demonstrative pronoun** may function as a subject, a subjective complement, a direct object, an indirect object, or an object of a preposition.

Demonstrative Pronouns

Singular	Plural	
this	these	(refers to someone or something that is near)
that	those	(refers to someone or something that is at a distance)

Remember that a pronoun replaces a noun. If the word *this, that, these,* or *those* appears with a noun in a sentence, then it is not a pronoun but an adjective.

Pronoun
Please move **that**.

Adjective
Please move **that** car.

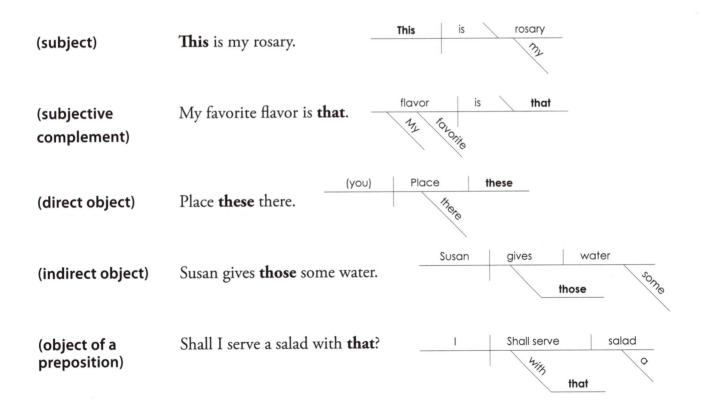

(subject) — This is my rosary.

(subjective complement) — My favorite flavor is **that**.

(direct object) — Place **these** there.

(indirect object) — Susan gives **those** some water.

(object of a preposition) — Shall I serve a salad with **that**?

Saint Thomas More, Pray for us! J.M.J. English 8 for Young Catholics

Lesson 26: PRONOUNS

Exercise 26A: On the lines to the right, write whether the italicized word in the sentence is a pronoun or an adjective.

1. *This* church has an early morning Mass. _____
2. *This* is the best way to begin one's day. _____
3. *This* time should be spent in close union with Christ. _____
4. *This* is the day the Lord has made, let us rejoice and be glad. _____
5. Is *that* your Holy Bible? _____
6. On *this* day, O beautiful Mother, we give thee our praise. _____
7. *These* bodies of ours are temples of the Holy Spirit. _____
8. *That* is why we should respect them and not sin. _____
9. *Those* are my spiritual books. _____
10. I leave *those* books in church so others can use them. _____

Exercise 26B: Circle the demonstrative pronouns in each sentence. On the lines to the right, write the function of that pronoun in the sentence.

1. My spiritual books are these. _____
2. Put the new missals with those. _____
3. Is this yours? _____
4. He showed those the way to eternal life. _____
5. Write your name on that. _____
6. This is my new friend. _____
7. I will never forget that. _____
8. The breakfast juices are these. _____
9. Our Lord grants these forgiveness. _____
10. Sam does not like those. _____

PRONOUNS

Lesson 27

Interrogative Pronouns

> An **interrogative pronoun** asks a question.

Interrogative Pronouns

	Case	
Refer to Persons		
who	nominative	used as a subject or subjective complement
whom	objective	used as a direct object or object of a preposition
Refer to Persons or Things		
which	nominative or objective	
whose (indicates possession)	nominative or objective	
Refers to Things		
what	nominative or objective	
Requests general information		
what	nominative or objective	

	Case	Function in the Sentence
Who will say Mass?	nominative	subject
It was **who**?	nominative	subjective complement
Whom did you see?	objective	direct object
Ralph gave **whom** the book?	objective	indirect object
For **whom** do they pray?	objective	object of a preposition
Which came first?	nominative	subject
In **which** shall we place the cards?	objective	object of a preposition
Whose will be first?	nominative	subject
Whose did they choose?	objective	direct object
What is in the bin?	nominative	subject
What did he bring with him?	objective	direct object
What happened?	nominative	subject
What do you think?	objective	direct object

Saint Thomas More, Pray for us!

Lesson 27 PRONOUNS

Exercise 27A: Circle the interrogative pronouns. On the lines to the right, write the function of each pronoun in the sentence and its case.

	Function	Case
1. Who made us?	_____	_____
2. For what did God make us?	_____	_____
3. What is heaven?	_____	_____
4. What must we do?	_____	_____
5. To whom does she teach algebra?	_____	_____
6. Which will you choose?	_____	_____
7. Who is our Good Shepherd?	_____	_____
8. Whose will you pick?	_____	_____
9. What is necessary?	_____	_____
10. What is the lesson from the parable?	_____	_____
11. Who are the three Persons in one God?	_____	_____
12. Which are the chief creatures of God?	_____	_____
13. To whom should we pray every day?	_____	_____
14. Who knows our every action and thought?	_____	_____
15. Who is always with us?	_____	_____
16. To whom did God give His only Son?	_____	_____
17. Which is the one true Church?	_____	_____
18. Who was the first pope appointed by Christ?	_____	_____
19. What is the particular judgment?	_____	_____
20. Whom will we meet in Heaven?	_____	_____

Exercise 27B: Diagram this sentence:
To whom did you give the coin?

PRONOUNS

Lesson 28

Relative Pronouns

> A **relative pronoun** is used in a complex sentence.
> A complex sentence is one that contains both an independent clause and a dependent clause.
> A clause is a part of a sentence that contains a subject and a predicate.
> The **relative pronoun** connects a dependent clause to the pronoun's antecedent in the independent clause.

Relative Pronouns

Refer to Persons	Case	Function in the Dependent Clause
who	nominative	used as a subject
whom	objective	used as a direct object, or an object of a preposition

Refer to Persons or Things	Case	Function in the Dependent Clause
that	nominative or objective	(same as above)
whose	(case does not apply)	used as a possessive adjective

Refers to Things	Case	Function in the Dependent Clause
which	nominative or objective	(same a above)

dependent clause

See the <u>man</u> **who** has told me my sins.
(The noun <u>man</u> in the independent clause is the <u>antecedent</u> of the relative pronoun **who**.)

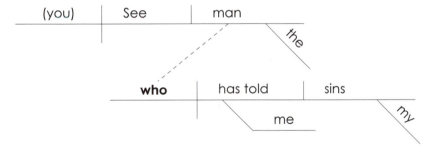

(subject)   Nazareth lies south of <u>Cana</u>, **which** is the site of Our Lord's first miracle.

dependent clause

(direct object)   The <u>One</u> **Whom** you seek has risen.

dependent clause

(object of a preposition)   This is My Beloved <u>Son</u>, in **Whom** I am well pleased.

Lesson 28: PRONOUNS

Exercise 28: Circle the correct relative pronoun and underline its antecedent. Write the function and the case of the relative pronoun in the dependent clause.

	Function	Case
Example: Christians, (who, **whom**) God loves, should thank God daily.	direct object	objective
1. Jesus is the One (Who, Whom) is to save His people.		
2. Mary will give birth to a Son (Who, Whom) is to save His people.		
3. Immanuel is a name (which, who) means "God-is-with-us."		
4. Jesus, (Who, Whom) we receive in Holy Communion, is our best Friend.		
5. Herod asked the wise men the exact date on (which, that) the star had appeared.		
6. The Wise Men traveled the road (who, that) led to Bethlehem.		
7. The house into (that, which) Jesus entered belonged to a Pharisee.		
8. A wise man (that, which) fears the Lord shuns evil.		
9. The Lord your God is the One to (Who, Whom) you must do homage.		
10. The woman (who, whom) the Pharisees had condemned was forgiven.		
11. Jesus celebrated Passover in Jerusalem, (who, which) is near His birth place, Bethlehem.		
12. This is My Son, in (Who, Whom) I am well pleased.		
13. Elizabeth is the cousin (who, whom) Mary visited.		
14. This story, (whom, which) I read last night, tells about the prodigal son.		
15. The people (which, that) walked in darkness have seen a great light.		

PRONOUNS

Lesson 29

Indefinite Pronouns

> An **indefinite pronoun** points to no specific person, place, or thing.

Indefinite Pronouns

These indefinite pronouns are **always singular**:

another	much	anybody	anyone	anything
each	one	everybody	everyone	everything
either	other	nobody	no one	nothing
neither		somebody	someone	something

These indefinite pronouns are **always plural**:

both	few	many	most	several	others

These indefinite pronouns may be **singular or plural**, depending on the noun they replace:

all	enough	none	some
any	more	same	such

> An **indefinite pronoun**
> —is in the third person, and
> —may function as a subject, a subjective complement, a direct object, an indirect object, or an object of a preposition.

(subject)	**Anybody** may lead the Rosary.	
(subjective complement)	There is **enough** for dinner.	
(direct object)	Mark remembered **something**.	
(indirect object)	Give **others** their due respect.	
(object of a preposition)	Grandma had a card for **each**.	

Saint Thomas More, Pray for us!   J.M.J.   English 8 for Young Catholics

Lesson 29: PRONOUNS

> When an **indefinite pronoun** functions as the **subject** of a sentence, the **verb** must agree in number (singular or plural) with the indefinite pronoun.

Singular	As for the choice of desserts, **either is** fine with me.
Plural	As for those desserts, **both are** fine with me.
Singular	**Everyone goes** to Confession at least once a month.
Plural	**Some go** to Mass every day.
Singular	**All remains** in your hands.
Plural	**All remain** at the parish hall.

Exercise 29A: Circle the correct verb(s) in each sentence.

1. All (wish, wishes) to go to the Christmas play.
2. I will take the van if anyone (need, needs) a ride.
3. Everyone (need, needs) Christ's grace to reach Heaven.
4. All (is, are) called to be perfect even as our Father in Heaven is.
5. Please send me some information, if any (is, are) available.
6. No one (reach, reaches) the Father except through Me.
7. Such (is, are) the consequences of a life well-lived.
8. If someone (arrive, arrives) early for Mass today, seat him up front.
9. I have two sisters; either (stay, stays) with me when my mom goes shopping.
10. Of these two dresses, neither (appeal, appeals) to me.
11. Both (arrive, arrives) early, but neither (are, is) prepared.
12. I would like some apples if any (is, are) ripe.
13. If anyone in the crowd (cheer, cheers) for the team, it will help.
14. Such (is, are) the power of God.

PRONOUNS

Lesson 29

When an **indefinite pronoun** is the **antecedent of a personal pronoun**, the personal pronoun must agree with the indefinite pronoun in number and gender.

Personal pronouns that have an **indefinite pronoun** as their antecedent:

	Indefinite Pronoun as Antecedent	Number	Gender	Personal Pronoun
Each claimed **he** left early.	Each	singular	masculine	he
One said her friend lent **her** the book.	One	singular	feminine	her
If **anything** is broken, **it** will be replaced.	anything	singular	neuter	it
Many came, but Joe did not know **them**.	Many	plural	masculine	them
When **both** arrived, **they** visited the chapel.	both	plural	masculine	they

When an **indefinite pronoun** is the **antecedent of a noun with a possessive adjective**, the possessive adjective must agree in number and gender with the indefinite pronoun.

Nouns with **possessive adjectives** that have an **indefinite pronoun** as their antecedent:

	Indefinite Pronoun as Antecedent	Number	Gender	Possessive Adjective
Neither had met **his** neighbor.	Neither	singular	masculine	his
Does **anyone** have **her** veil?	anyone	singular	feminine	her
Each has **his** own boat.	Each	singular	masculine	his
Someone is wearing **her** skirt.	Someone	singular	feminine	her
Few brought **their** dresses to the rehearsal.	Few	plural	feminine	their
Most had prepared **their** answers.	Most	plural	masculine	their
We had met **some**; we knew **their** parents.	some	plural	masculine	their

Saint Thomas More, Pray for us! J.M.J. English 8 for Young Catholics

Lesson 29: PRONOUNS

Exercise 29B: Circle the correct personal pronoun in each sentence.

1. If either should ask, tell (him, them) I'll be right back.
2. None is so brave that (he, they) will confront the giant.
3. When some boils over the pot, wipe (it, them) up.
4. As soon as some fall out of the tree, pick (it, them) up.
5. Someone was at the door, but Dominic did not recognize (him, them).
6. I saw none, and (he, they) did not see me.
7. Few had hymnals, so (he, they) shared with others.
8. Neither said (she, they) will be available to babysit tomorrow.
9. Somebody may ask directions, and you will have to help (him, them).
10. There remained few on the platter, and Barbara ate (it, them).

Exercise 29C: Circle the correct possessive adjective in each sentence.

1. Father asked everybody to hand in (his, their) donation for the missions.
2. Both showed up with (his, their) books.
3. Each of the children of Fatima brought (his, their) rosary.
4. Somebody gave me (his, their) own rosary by mistake.
5. Some will ride to the March for Life in (his, their) own cars.
6. Everybody wants (his, their) children to reach Heaven.
7. Each of the singers in the choir sewed (his, their) own robe.
8. Many of them offered (his, their) lives to Christ as martyrs in the Colosseum.
9. Both cheered (his, their) children on at the soccer match.
10. No one could find (his, their) car in the parking lot.

CHAPTER 3

ADJECTIVES

ADJECTIVES

ADJECTIVES

Chapter Outline

CHAPTER THREE

I. **Types of adjectives**
   A. Descriptive
      1. Proper vs. common
      2. Position in sentence
   B. Limiting
      1. Articles: *the, a, an*
      2. Numeral adjectives: *one, two, three, …* (or *1, 2, 3, …*); *first, second, third, …*
      3. Pronominal
         a. Demonstrative: *this, that, these, those*
         b. Possessive: *my, your, his, her, its, our, their, whose*
         c. Interrogative: *which, what, whose*
         d. Indefinite: *another   both   all*
                         each   few   any
                         either   many   most
                         every   several no
                         much   some
                         neither   such

II. **Degrees of comparison of adjectives**
III. **Correct use of adjectives**
   A. *Fewer* and *less*
   B. Repetition of the article
   C. Words used as adjectives and nouns

Saint Thomas More, Pray for us! J.M.J. English 8 for Young Catholics

Lesson 30: ADJECTIVES

Diagrams help us to visualize the function of adjectives in a sentence.

    article descriptive   numeral   numeral article   attributive adjectives

1. The American team has won first place for five years in a row.

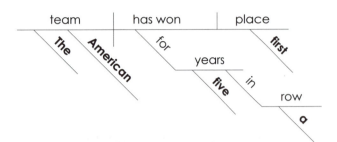

    possessive   demonstrative   attributive adjectives

2. My brothers and yours are participants in that one.

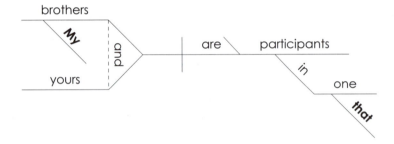

   demonstrative descriptive   demonstrative   descriptive

3. This event is popular and well-attended, and it makes those boys nervous.

4. Which one will be fastest?

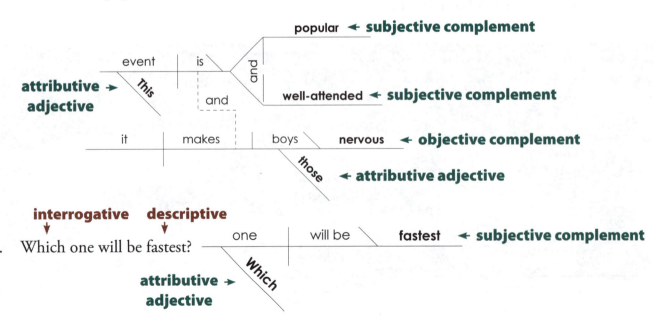

60   English 8 for Young Catholics   J.M.J.   *Saint Thomas More, Pray for us!*

ADJECTIVES

Lesson 30

Descriptive Adjectives

> An **adjective** is the part of speech that describes or limits a noun or pronoun.

> The two types of adjectives are **descriptive** and **limiting**.
> A **descriptive adjective** describes a noun or a pronoun.
> A **limiting adjective** points out a person or a thing or shows a number.

> Kinds of **descriptive adjectives**: **proper** and **common**.
> A **proper descriptive adjective** is usually formed from a proper noun.
> A **common descriptive adjective** is any adjective that expresses a common quality of a noun or pronoun.

Proper adjectives   The **American** flag waved in the breeze, and the **Nazi** soldiers faltered.
Common adjectives   She walked down the **narrow** path toward the **empty** house.

Exercise 30: Circle the descriptive adjectives in each sentence. Above each adjective that you circle, write P for a proper adjective or C for a common adjective.

1. St. Sebastian was the son of wealthy parents.
2. St. Sebastian was killed by the Roman emperor because he was a Christian.
3. Mother Teresa cared for the sick people of the back streets.
4. St. Methodius invented the Slav alphabet.
5. When Juan Diego opened his old tilma, the bishop saw a beautiful image of Mary.
6. The chocolate cake for his Confirmation had a large white dove on it.
7. St. Patrick had a vivid dream of the Irish people begging him to return.
8. On this mountain, God is preparing a rich banquet.
9. May the words of God not fall on deaf ears and frozen hearts!
10. God was not in the loud noise but in the gentle breeze.

Lesson 31: ADJECTIVES

Position of Adjectives

Adjectives may occupy different **positions in a sentence**.

The usual position of an adjective is before the noun or pronoun it describes. When an adjective is in this position, it is an **attributive adjective**.
When an adjective follows and completes a linking verb, it is a **subjective complement**.
When an adjective follows and explains a direct object, it is an **objective complement**.

Attributive	The child has **blue** eyes, **blond** hair, and a **beautiful** voice. The **new** store sells **Danish** furniture.
Subjective complement	Their parents will be **proud** to attend the graduation. Frank seems **happy** with the French tutor.
Objective complement	The children made their parents **proud**. The announcement left them **confused**.

Exercise 31: Circle the descriptive adjectives in each sentence. Above each adjective that you circle, write AA for an attributive adjective, SC for a subjective complement and OC for an objective complement.

1. Enter by the narrow gate; the road that leads to destruction is wide.
2. Grace makes the soul holy.
3. God is omnipotent and omniscient.
4. In grassy meadows, He lets me lie; by tranquil streams, He leads me.
5. He set my feet on solid rock and made my footsteps firm.
6. We consider Sam's attitude excellent.
7. Colorful butterflies dot the vast field.
8. Our Lady appeared radiant in her resplendent blue and white robe.
9. Mary was happy, but Martha seemed troubled.
10. Poor roads made the journey difficult.

ADJECTIVES

Lesson 32

Limiting Adjectives: Articles and Numeral Adjectives

> A **limiting adjective** either points out a person or thing, or shows number.
> **Types of limiting adjectives**: articles, numeral adjectives, and pronominal adjectives.

Articles

> The **articles** *the*, *a*, and *an* are used as adjectives in a sentence.
> The article *the*
>   – is a definite article,
>   – is used to point out particular persons or things, and
>   – may modify either singular or plural nouns or pronouns.
>
> The articles *a* and *an*
>   – are indefinite articles,
>   – are used to show any one of a number of persons or things, and
>   – may modify only singular nouns or pronouns.
>
> Use *a* before a word that begins with a consonant.
> Use *an* before a word that begins with a vowel.

The Eucharist was exposed for adoration, and **an** adorer knelt in prayer.
Together, **the** artists painted **a** huge mural.

Numeral Adjectives

> A **numeral adjective** shows exact number.
> The **numeral adjectives** are *one, two, three…* and *first, second, third…*

Exercise 32: Circle all the articles and the numeral adjectives in each sentence.

1. An altar boy placed the cruet on the table near the altar.
2. The tallest of the girls in the choir is my sister.
3. The two teams reached an agreement about a starting time for the twelve games.
4. The four boys went through an entryway on the seventeenth floor.
5. It was the first time they took a Spanish course together.

Lesson 33: ADJECTIVES

Limiting Adjectives: Pronominal Adjectives

> A **pronominal adjective** is a word that modifies a noun by
> – **pointing out** a person or thing,
> – **showing possession or ownership**, or
> – **asking a question**.

Pronominal Adjectives

Demonstrative Adjectives	Possessive Adjectives	Interrogative Adjectives	Indefinite Adjectives
this, that, these, those	*my, your, his, her, its our, their, whose*	*which, what, whose*	*each, either, neither, no, every, any, all, another, both, few, many, most, much, several, some, such*

> We call these words **pronominal adjectives** because, when they have a different function in a sentence, they are pronouns. (See the chapter on pronouns).
>
> All the pronominal adjectives can be used as pronouns except *my, our, your, their,* and *every*.
>
> Be careful not to confuse pronominal adjectives with pronouns!
> An adjective modifies a noun or pronoun. **Adjective** **This** guitar belongs to Jim.
> A pronoun takes the place of a noun. **Pronoun** **This** belongs to Jim.

Exercise 33: Identify the words in italics by writing Adjective or Pronoun on the lines on the right.

1. *This* house is God's house too. _____
2. Please hand him *his* towel. _____
3. *Which* would you like, the brown cap or the blue one? _____
4. *Each* spiritual book has a name on the inside cover. _____
5. May I borrow *your* pen? _____
6. Do you know *much* about the planet Venus? _____
7. *That* is one for the record books. _____
8. We cheered the team with *much* gusto. _____

ADJECTIVES

Lesson 34

Limiting Adjectives: Pronominal Adjectives: Demonstrative

A **demonstrative adjective** modifies a noun by **pointing out** a person, place, or thing.

Demonstrative Adjectives

Singular	Plural	
this	these	(for persons or things that are near)
that	those	(for persons or things that are at a distance)

Singular demonstrative adjectives modify singular nouns or pronouns.
Plural demonstrative adjectives modify plural nouns.
Plural demonstrative adjectives do not modify pronouns.

Do not confuse **demonstrative adjectives** with **demonstrative pronouns**.
An **adjective** modifies a noun or a pronoun.   A **pronoun** takes the place of a noun.
 This <u>song</u> is my favorite.   **This** is my favorite.
 Those <u>roses</u> are gorgeous!   **Those** are gorgeous.

Demonstrative Adjectives
I repainted **this** statue.
Tomorrow, I will do **that** one.

Demonstrative Pronouns
I repainted **this**.
Tomorrow, I will do **that**.

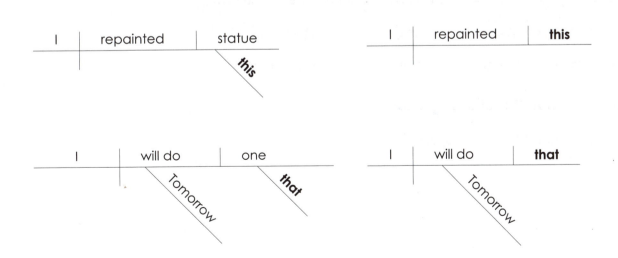

Saint Thomas More, Pray for us! J.M.J. English 8 for Young Catholics **65**

Lesson 34: ADJECTIVES

Exercise 34A: Circle the demonstrative adjective in each sentence.

1. We bought that statue of Our Lady of Fatima during our pilgrimage.
2. We made sure to have these rosaries blessed while we were there.
3. Let us offer this prayer for an end to abortion.
4. These Sorrowful Mysteries are usually said on Tuesdays and Fridays.
5. To you we send up our sighs, mourning and weeping in this valley of tears.

Exercise 34B: Fill in each blank with the correct demonstrative adjective. Use the word in parentheses to determine the correct adjective to use. Be sure that each agrees in number with the noun it modifies.

1. (Near) _____ sacred season, called Advent, became universal in the ninth century.
2. (Near) During _____ time, we prepare for the coming of our Savior, Jesus Christ.
3. (Near) Every time you make a sacrifice, you may put one of _____ straws in the manger.
4. (Distant) _____ sacrifices will make a soft bed for the Christ Child.
5. (Distant) I shall never forget _____ years with my brothers and sisters.

Exercise 34C: Circle the demonstrative adjective and the demonstrative pronoun in each sentence. Above each word you circle, write A for an adjective or P for a pronoun.

1. May I borrow these rosaries and those for the group?
2. I made those from this recipe.
3. I love these prayers, but those on the Advent calendar are my favorite.
4. This is the spot where Juan Diego built the chapel to that special Lady.
5. These sacrifices are not as great as that of the crucifixion of Jesus.

Exercise 34D: Diagram the following sentence:

On that joyful third day, Our Lord appeared glorious.

ADJECTIVES

Lesson 35

Limiting Adjectives: Pronominal Adjectives: Possessive

A **possessive adjective** modifies a noun by **showing possession or ownership**.

Possessive Adjectives

Singular	Plural
my	*our*
your	*your*
his	*their*
her	*whose*
its	

Do not confuse **possessive adjectives** with **possessive pronouns**.

An adjective modifies a noun or a pronoun
My <u>coat</u> is new.
Your <u>roses</u> are gorgeous!

A pronoun takes the place of a noun.
Mine is new.
Yours are gorgeous.

Possessive Adjectives

His <u>rosary</u> is on **her** <u>bureau</u> with hers.
This one is **your** <u>rosary</u>.
Our <u>van</u> held **their** <u>equipment</u> and ours.

Possessive Pronouns

His is on her bureau with **hers**.
This is **yours**.
Ours held **theirs** and **ours**.

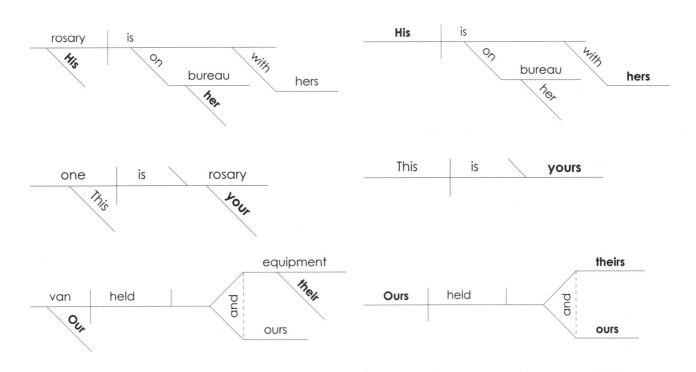

Saint Thomas More, Pray for us! — J.M.J. — English 8 for Young Catholics

Lesson 35: ADJECTIVES

Exercise 35A: Circle all the possessive adjectives in the following sentences.

1. My rosary is blue, and hers is clear glass.
2. Their rosaries are still on the statue.
3. We pray the Rosary before our bedtime.
4. Turn, then, most gracious Advocate, your eyes of mercy toward us.
5. After this our exile, show unto us the Blessed Fruit of your womb, Jesus.
6. The list of our intentions and theirs always seems to grow.
7. My new book of saints' stories is in our den next to yours.
8. They offered their sacrifices for the poor souls in Purgatory.
9. A yellow butterfly opened its wings to fly away.
10. We went back to get his cap and her sweater and mine.

Exercise 35B: Diagram the following sentences:

1. The tree with our best apples is yours.

2. Its strong limbs can hold their weight.

ADJECTIVES

Lesson 36

Limiting Adjectives: Pronominal Adjectives: Interrogative

> An **interrogative adjective** modifies a noun by **asking a question**.

Interrogative Adjectives
which, what, whose

Do not confuse **interrogative adjectives** with **interrogative pronouns**.
An adjective modifies a noun or pronoun.   A pronoun takes the place of a noun.
   Which <u>one</u> is first?   **Which** is first?
   What <u>mystery</u> do you like?   **What** do you like?
   Whose <u>name</u> will they choose?   **Whose** will they choose?

Interrogative Adjectives   **Interrogative Pronouns**

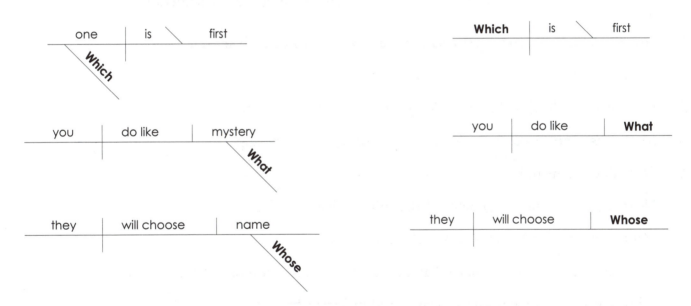

Exercise 36: Circle the interrogative adjectives in each sentence.

1. What color is the vestment used by the priest during Lent?

2. In which mysteries do we recall the sufferings of Christ?

3. May I see which one you bought?

4. In what town was Christ born?

5. Do you know whose name is next on the list for adoration?

Lesson 37: ADJECTIVES

Pronominal Adjectives: Indefinite

> An **indefinite adjective** refers to **no particular** person, place, or thing.

Indefinite Adjectives

Used with Singular Nouns	Used with Plural Nouns	Used with Singular or Plural Nouns	
another	*both*	*all*	*no*
each	*few*	*any*	*some*
either	*many*	*most*	*such*
every	*several*		
much			
neither			

Each child offers an intention.
Several persons joined us.
Some people pray the Rosary at church.
Some smell of incense remains after each Benediction.

Exercise 37: Circle the correct words (singular or plural) in each sentence.

1. The rosary is led by either (parent, parents).
2. In some (church, churches) we may go to adoration at any time.
3. Mary asks people to pray the Rosary every (time, times) she appears.
4. Dad added some (oil, oils) to the engine.
5. Neither (mother, mothers) believed the children had seen Our Lady.
6. Most (time, times), unbelievers simply turned away.
7. Each (apparition, apparitions) at Fatima was on the thirteenth day of the month.
8. All (intention, intentions) have been placed in Mary's hands.
9. This glass will hold the most (juice, juices).
10. Mom told neither (boy, boys) about the surprise.

ADJECTIVES

Lesson 38

Degrees of Comparison of Adjectives

> Adjectives may be used to express **degrees of comparison** of quality, quantity, or value. Most adjectives express three degrees of comparison: **positive**, **comparative**, and **superlative**.

> The **positive** degree
> – is the adjective itself,
> – shows quality, quantity, or value,
> – shows no comparison, and
> – is the basis for forming the comparative and superlative degrees of comparison.

Joe is **tall**.   (Joe is not compared with anyone.)

> The **comparative** degree
> – shows quality, quantity, or value **in greater or lesser degree**, and
> – is used when speaking of **two** persons or things.

Tom is **taller** than Joe.   (Tom is compared with Joe.)
The boys are **taller** than the girls.   (The group of boys is compared with the group of girls.)

> The **superlative** degree
> – shows quality, quantity, or value **in the greatest or least degree**, and
> – is used when speaking of **three or more** persons or things.

Mr. Smith is the **tallest** in the room. (Mr. Smith is compared with every person in the room.)

Adjectives in the positive degree form the comparative degree and the superlative degree in different ways.

Positive	Comparative	Superlative
few	fewer	fewest
flat	flatter	flattest
brave	braver	bravest
funny	funnier	funniest
famous	more / less famous	most / least famous
good	better	best

Lesson 38: ADJECTIVES

Rules for Forming the Degrees of Comparison of Adjectives

1. One-syllable adjectives usually form the comparative degree by adding *er* and the superlative degree by adding *est*.

Positive	Comparative	Superlative
small	smaller	smallest
long	longer	longest
soft	softer	softest

2. Some one-syllable adjectives that end in a single consonant preceded by a single vowel in the positive degree double the consonant before adding *er* and *est*.

Positive	Comparative	Superlative
hot	hotter	hottest
big	bigger	biggest
sad	sadder	saddest

3. One-syllable adjectives that end in *e* in the positive degree form the comparative degree by adding *r* and the superlative degree by adding *st*.

Positive	Comparative	Superlative
large	larger	largest
rare	rarer	rarest
fine	finer	finest

4. If the positive degree of the adjective ends in *y* preceded by a consonant, change the *y* to *i* before adding *er* for the comparative degree and *est* for the superlative degree.

Positive	Comparative	Superlative
weary	wearier	weariest
happy	happier	happiest
silly	sillier	silliest

ADJECTIVES

Lesson 38

5. Most two-syllable adjectives and those of three or more syllables form the comparative degree by adding *more* or *less* before the adjective.
They form the superlative degree by adding *most* or *least* before the adjective.

Positive	Comparative	Superlative
industrious	more / less industrious	most / least industrious
thoughtful	more / less thoughtful	most / least thoughtful
flexible	more / less flexible	most / least flexible

6. Certain adjectives form the comparative and superlative degrees **by changing the word completely**.

Positive	Comparative	Superlative
little	less	least
bad	worse	worst
good	better	best
many, much	more	most
far	farther	farthest
*	further	furthest
*	inner	innermost, inmost
*	outer	outermost, outmost
*	upper	uppermost, upmost

* These adjectives have no positive form.

7. Some adjectives denote quality, quantity, or value that have no comparison. These are words such as **dead, eternal, supreme, perfect, ultimate, absolute, infinite,** and **perpendicular**.

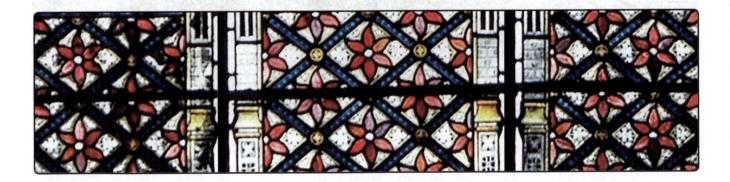

Lesson 38: ADJECTIVES

Exercise 38: Write the comparative degree and the superlative degree of each adjective. If no comparison applies, write NONE.

Positive	Comparative	Superlative
Example: tall	taller	tallest
1. dry		
2. thoughtful		
3. good		
4. knowledgeable		
5. ultimate		
6. fancy		
7. many		
8. bad		
9. infinite		
10. much		

ADJECTIVES

Lesson 39

Correct Use of Adjectives: *Fewer* and *Less*

> The **comparative degree** of an adjective shows quality, quantity, or value in greater or lesser degree, and is used when speaking of two persons or things.
> The comparative degree of *few* is *fewer*, and it is used when comparing **number**.
> The comparative degree of *little* is *less*, and it is used when comparing **quantity**.

In our family, there are **fewer** boys than girls.   (compares the **number** of children)
We have had **less** rain this summer than usual.   (compares the **quantity** of rain)

Exercise 39: Fill in each blank with the correct comparative adjective, *fewer* or *less*.

1. After Father Martin's advice, _____ people left Mass after Communion.

2. Jesus spent _____ time preaching in Nazareth than in other towns.

3. We bought _____ gifts this year than last year.

4. When he checked the wood stove, there was _____ fire than the night before.

5. We should spend more time reading books and _____ time watching television.

6. She made _____ trips to the store this week.

7. _____ people will eat those because they have _____ sugar in them.

8. _____ miracles were worked by Jesus in His hometown than elsewhere.

9. This was because the people there had _____ faith in Him.

10. The _____ occasions of sin we encounter, the better off we will be.

11. Francis said _____ prayers than Joseph.

12. There are _____ days in Advent than in Lent.

13. In order to reach Heaven, I must have _____ love for myself than for Christ.

14. The saints put _____ trust in their own strength than in God's.

15. We should not have _____ concern for venial sins, since they can become a habit.

Saint Thomas More, Pray for us!   J.M.J.   English 8 for Young Catholics   75

Lesson 40: ADJECTIVES

Correct Use of Adjectives: Repetition of the Article

> The single use or the repetition of the articles *the*, *a*, and *an* before nouns in a sentence changes the meaning of the sentence.
> Place the article **before both nouns** to show that the nouns are taken **separately**.
> Place the article **before the first noun only** to show that the nouns are taken **together**.

I know **the** president and **the** secretary.
There is **a** sergeant and **a** lieutenant.

The articles *the* and *a* are placed before both nouns to indicate two separate people holding two positions.

I know **the** president and secretary.
There is **a** secretary and treasurer.

The articles *the* and *a* are placed before the first noun only to indicate one person holding two offices.

Exercise 40: In the following sentences, write an article in the blank if one is required. If no article is necessary, put a dash (—) in the blank.

1. We are waiting for the altar boy and _____ lector since they are both from our family.
2. The priest and _____ seminarian both came over for dinner.
3. God, the Creator and _____ Provider of us all, inspired the saints.
4. The bus driver and _____ guide both agreed that St. Peter's was the best place to go.
5. The hands and _____ feet of Jesus are kissed on the crucifix on Good Friday.
6. The Companion and _____ Friend of all Christians is Jesus Christ.
7. The pope has a yellow and _____ white flag.
8. A red and _____ white car were sold today.
9. We prayed to Saint Agnes, the patron and _____ helper of the Children of Mary.
10. The athletes and _____ soldiers both turn to Saint Sebastian for aid.
11. The captain and _____ soldiers helped to defend the freedom of our country.
12. The alto and _____ tenor complement each other while singing.
13. The shepherds and _____ Wise Men came to adore Jesus.
14. A boy and _____ girl each received an academic award.
15. St. Thomas More was a lawyer and _____ statesman.

ADJECTIVES

Lesson 41

Words Used as Adjectives and Nouns

Some words may be used as adjectives or as nouns.
The word is a **noun** if it names a person, place, or thing.
The word is an **adjective** if it describes or limits a noun.

Noun
The **iron** is very hot.
He made the statue from **clay**.

Adjective
The **iron** pot was left on the stove.
The **clay** statue was beautiful.

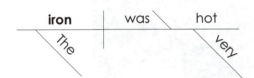

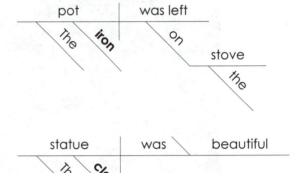

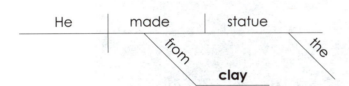

Exercise 41: In the space provided, write whether the word in italics is a noun or an adjective.

1. The *Catholic* knelt reverently at the Shrine of St. Peter. _____
2. The sun glistened on the *still* water of the pond. _____
3. The scientist developed a new *chemical* to improve our drinking water. _____
4. Jesus tells us not to worry about *food* to eat, because God will provide it. _____
5. Matthew is one of the authors of the *Gospels*. _____
6. The nuns in the convent made the *communion* hosts. _____
7. The *fruit* tree became withered because of drought. _____
8. St. Peter was put in a *prison* in Rome. _____
9. We can build our lives on *firm* ground by frequenting the sacraments. _____
10. The *prison* guard was converted by St. Peter. _____
11. He made sure to buy a *safe* wood stove. _____
12. They were not to eat the *fruit* of the tree of good and evil. _____

Lesson 41 — ADJECTIVES

CHAPTER 4

VERBS

VERBS

VERBS

Chapter Outline

CHAPTER FOUR

I. **Verbs and sentences**
II. **Verb phrases**
III. **Kinds of verbs**
   A. According to form
      1. Regular
      2. Irregular
   B. According to use
      1. Action verbs
         a. Transitive
         b. Intransitive
      2. Being and state of being verbs (linking verbs)
IV. **Qualities of verbs**
   A. Voice
      1. Active
      2. Passive
   B. Tense
      1. Simple tenses
         a. Present
         b. Past
         c. Future
      2. Perfect tenses
         a. Present perfect
         b. Past perfect
         c. Future perfect
   C. Mood
      1. Indicative
      2. Imperative
   D. Person
      1. First
      2. Second
      3. Third
   E. Number
      1. Singular
      2. Plural
V. **Subject/predicate agreement**
   A. Person and number
   B. Compound subjects
      1. Connected by *and*
      2. Compound subjects preceded by *each, every, many a,* or *no*
      3. Compound subjects preceded by *neither/nor* or *either/or*
   C. Collective noun subjects
VI. **Words used as verbs and nouns**

Saint Thomas More, Pray for us!   J.M.J.

Lesson 42: VERBS

Verbs and Sentences

> A **verb** is the part of speech that expresses **action**, **being**, or **state of being**.
>
> A verb that expresses **action** is an **action verb**.
>
> A verb that expresses **being** states a **condition** rather than an action. It is any form of the verb *be*.
>
> A verb that expresses **state of being** states a **condition** rather than an action; it is any verb that may be replaced by a form of the verb *be*.
>
> Verbs that express **being** or **state of being** are **linking verbs**.

> A **sentence** expresses a **complete thought**.
>
> In order to express a complete thought, a sentence must contain a **verb**.
>
> A group of words that has **no verb** is not a sentence. It is a **sentence fragment**.
>
> A **verb by itself** can be a complete thought, that is, a **sentence**. (The subject is understood; the subject is *you*.)
>
> When a **verb** is used in a sentence, it is a **predicate**.

Action	John **baptized** Jesus in the Jordan.
Action	**Run!**
Being	Jesus **is** the Founder of the Catholic Church.
State of Being	Sara **looked** happy at the party.

Exercise 42: Put a check mark before each of the following that is a sentence.

____ 1. I will go to Confession often.
____ 2. The miracles of Jesus, Our Savior.
____ 3. Proceed to the left.
____ 4. The rest to the right.
____ 5. Many saints from the city of Rome.
____ 6. Jesus wept.
____ 7. My father, our teacher of science.
____ 8. Excuse me.
____ 9. No, never!
____ 10. Remain silent.
____ 11. Pray for us.
____ 12. She shook her head.
____ 13. Are you sure?
____ 14. The narrow path to Heaven.
____ 15. Be prepared.
____ 16. Christians at the March for Life.
____ 17. When?
____ 18. God, our Father in Heaven.
____ 19. Jesus cleansed the Temple.
____ 20. Jesus in the Garden of Gethsemane.

VERBS

Lesson 43

Verb Phrases

> A **verb** is the part of speech that expresses action, being, or state of being.
>
> A **verb phrase**
> — is a **verb** that is made up of two or more words,
> — includes a **main verb** and one or more **helping verbs**,
> — functions as a **single verb**.

Common Helping Verbs

am	be	do	has	may	shall	can
is	being	does	have	might	will	could
are	been	did	had	must	should	would
was						
were						

Can we ever fully **grasp** the great depth of God's love for us?
You eventually **would have arrived** on the other side.
The children **will have been taught** the cardinal virtues by Sunday.
You **will be** fishers of men.

Diagrams demonstrate that verb phrases are made up of more than one verb, and that they are used as a single verb.

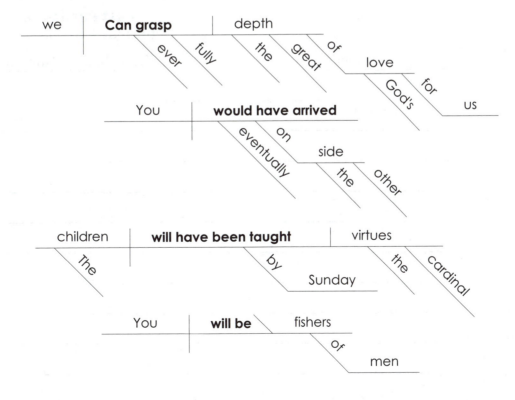

Saint Thomas More, Pray for us!   J.M.J.   English 8 for Young Catholics

Lesson 44: VERBS

Kinds of Verbs According to Form: Regular Verbs

There are two **kinds of verbs** according to **form**: **regular** and **irregular**. A verb is regular or irregular depending on the way it forms its principal parts. The **principal parts of a verb** are the **present**, the **past**, and the **past participle**.

The past and past participle parts of a **regular verb** have *d* or *ed* added to the present. Some regular verbs that end in a consonant double the consonant before adding *ed*. The past participle is always a verb phrase. It is the main verb preceded by the helping verb *have*, *has*, or *had*.

Forms of the regular verbs *save*, *retain*, and *step* in their principal parts:

Principal parts	Present	Past	Past Participle
Verb Forms	save	save**d**	have, has, or had save**d**
Verb Forms	retain	retain**ed**	have, has, or had retain**ed**
Verb Forms	step	step**ped**	have, has, or had step**ped**

Exercise 44: In the blanks, write the correct form of each verb in its principal parts.

Present	Past	Past Participle (include *have*, *has*, *had*)
Example: arrive	arrived	have, has, had arrived
1. live		
2. explain		
3. trip		
4. delay		
5. adore		
6. bless		
7. compose		
8. diagram		
9. remember		
10. start		

VERBS

Lesson 45

Kinds of Verbs According to Form: Irregular Verbs

> The principal parts of an **irregular verb do not** have *d* or *ed* added to the present. Although no general rules apply, the **form of most irregular verbs** changes in its principal parts.
> The past participle is always a verb phrase that includes the helping verb *have*, *has*, or *had*.

Forms of the irregular verbs *run* and *ride* in their principal parts

Principal parts	Present	Past	Past Participle
Verb Forms	run	ran	have, has, or had run
Verb Forms	ride	rode	have, has, or had ridden

There are no general rules for forming the past and the past participle of **irregular verbs**.

Below is a list of the past and the past participle of some common **irregular verbs**. Review these verbs so that you may use them correctly when you speak and write.

PRESENT	PAST	PAST PARTICIPLE (with *have*, *has*, or *had*)
am (is, are)	was, were	been
awake	awaked, awoke	awaked, awoken
beat	beat	beat, beaten
begin	began	begun
bend	bent	bent
bet	bet	bet
bind	bound	bound
bite	bit	bitten
blow	blew	blown
break	broke	broken
bring	brought	brought
build	built	built
burn	burned, burnt	burned, burnt
burst	burst	burst
catch	caught	caught
choose	chose	chosen
come	came	come
creep	crept	crept
do	did	done
draw	drew	drawn
dream	dreamed, dreamt	dreamed, dreamt
drink	drank	drunk
drive	drove	driven

Lesson 45: VERBS

PRESENT	PAST	PAST PARTICIPLE
dwell	dwelt, dwelled	dwelt, dwelled
eat	ate	eaten
fall	fell	fallen
find	found	found
flee	fled	fled
fly	flew	flown
forget	forgot	forgotten
freeze	froze	frozen
give	gave	given
go	went	gone
grow	grew	grown
hang	hung	hung
have	had	had
hide	hid	hidden, hid
hold	held	held
hurt	hurt	hurt
keep	kept	kept
kneel	knelt, kneeled	knelt, kneeled
knit	knit, knitted	knit, knitted
know	knew	known
lay	laid	laid
lead	led	led
leave	left	left
lend	lent	lent
let	let	let
lie (recline)	lay	lain
light	lighted, lit	lighted, lit
lose	lost	lost
make	made	made
mean	meant	meant
meet	met	met
read	read	read
ride	rode	ridden
ring	rang	rung
rise	rose	risen
run	ran	run
say	said	said
see	saw	seen
seek	sought	sought
set	set	set
shake	shook	shaken
show	showed	shown, showed
sing	sang	sung
sink	sank	sunk
sit	sat	sat
sleep	slept	slept
slide	slid	slid, slidden
smell	smelled	smelled
sow	sowed	sown, sowed

VERBS

Lesson 45

PRESENT	PAST	PAST PARTICIPLE
speak	spoke	spoken
spend	spent	spent
spill	spilled, spilt	spilled, spilt
stand	stood	stood
steal	stole	stolen
stick	stuck	stuck
sting	stung	stung
stride	strode	stridden
swim	swam	swum
teach	taught	taught
tear	tore	torn
throw	threw	thrown
wake	waked, woke	waked, woken
wear	wore	worn
weave	wove	woven
win	won	won
wind	wound	wound
wring	wrung	wrung
write	wrote	written

A few verbs do not have all the principal parts. They are *shall*, *will*, *can*, *may*, *must*, *ought*, and *beware*.

Saint Thomas More, Pray for us!   J.M.J.   English 8 for Young Catholics

Lesson 45: VERBS

Exercise 45: Fill in the blanks with the correct form (the past or the past participle) of the verb at the left of each sentence.

ride 1. Saul _____ towards Damascus to persecute the Christians.

know 2. He should have _____ that God would stop him.

teach 3. Mother Teresa _____ people by her good example.

fight 4. I have _____ the good fight.

light 5. The star _____ the sky over Bethlehem.

seek 6. The three Wise Men _____ the Infant King, Jesus.

come 7. They had _____ from a faraway land.

sink 8. Herod's heart _____ as he listened to the Magi.

write 9. Pope Paul VI _____ the encyclical letter *Humanae Vitae*. (*Of Human Life*)

sing 10. The choir _____ the song they had prepared for the Holy Father.

sing 11. They had _____ it all week.

know 12. Our Lord had _____ Peter would deny Him three times.

kneel 13. We _____ in front of the Blessed Sacrament in adoration.

lay 14. They _____ St. Cecilia's body in the catacombs in 117.

find 15. Others discovered her body in 817 and _____ it incorrupt.

see 16. Many pilgrims have _____ it in the Basilica of Saint Cecilia in Rome.

go 17. St. Therese of the Child Jesus never _____ to the missions.

do 18. Despite this, she _____ become the patroness of foreign missions.

make 19. By the time of her death, she had _____ many sacrifices and spent much time in prayer.

choose 20. I hope that I have _____ God's will over my own.

VERBS

Lesson 46

Irregular Verbs *Lie* and *Lay*; *Rise* and *Raise*

> The verbs **lie** and **lay** and **rise** and **raise** can be confusing. It is important to learn them well in order to use them correctly in speech and in writing.

Present	Past	Past Participle	Definition	Is there a receiver of the action?
lie	lay	have, has, had lain	to recline; to rest	never
lay	laid	have, has, had laid	to put, place, or position	always
rise	rose	have, has, had risen	to go up; to get up; to increase in size	never
raise	raised	have, has, had raised	to lift	always

Exercise 46: Circle the correct form of the verb in the parentheses. When there is a receiver of the action, underline it.

1. Jesus told His apostles that He would (rise, raise) on the third day.
2. Jesus had (risen, raised) Lazarus from the dead.
3. St. Stephen (lay, laid) down his life for Christ.
4. The incorrupt body of Saint Bernadette (lies, lays) in the Chapel of St. Joseph at Lourdes.
5. Joseph of Arimathaea (lay, laid) the body of Jesus in the tomb.
6. We (lay, laid) the scapulars on the church table for people to take.
7. Last night, we (lay, laid) wide awake during the thunderstorm.
8. After Mom kneaded the bread, she placed it on the counter so that it could (rise, raise).
9. Our dog likes to (lie, lay) on a soft pillow.
10. Mom gently (lies, lays) the baby in his crib.
11. The sun had (risen, raised) by the time we (raised, rose) from our beds.
12. Have they (risen, raised) the curtain on the stage yet?
13. Has the crew (lain, laid) the foundation for the new chapel?
14. The cost of vegetables has (risen, raised) significantly since we had that drought.
15. (Lie, lay) down and (lie, lay) your head on this pillow.

Lesson 47: VERBS

Kinds of Verbs According to Use: Action Verbs
Transitive and Intransitive

> A **transitive** verb expresses an **action that passes to a receiver**.
> The **receiver** of the action may be the **subject** or the **direct object**.

Transitive verb: the receiver of the action is the <u>subject</u>.

  The <u>Mass</u> **is sung** by the choir.
  The <u>sermon</u> **is preached**.

Transitive verb: the receiver of the action is the <u>direct object</u>.

  The choir **sings** the <u>Mass</u>.
  Father Roy **preaches** the <u>sermon</u>.

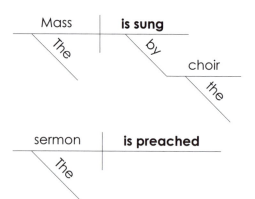

> An **intransitive verb** expresses an **action for which there is no receiver**.

  Intransitive verb (no receiver of the action)
  The Mass **starts** at ten.
  The choir **sings**.
  Father Roy **preaches**.

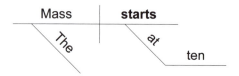

VERBS

Lesson 47

Exercise 47: Circle the verbs in each sentence. On the lines to the right, write T for a transitive verb and I for an intransitive verb.

1. Many of the Jews accepted Christianity, and Jesus as the promised Redeemer. _____
2. Christianity spread throughout the known world. _____
3. I have fought the good fight. _____
4. Mother Teresa worked tirelessly with the poor. _____
5. Peter and Paul both were killed around A. D. 67. _____
6. In the first century, the Church flourished despite the loss of its two greatest leaders, St. Peter and St. Paul. _____
7. The Church survived even with the death of many of its members. _____
8. Paul was taken to Rome. _____
9. Stephen worked great wonders among the people. _____
10. St. Stephen, the first martyr, spoke with great wisdom. _____
11. The Church was founded by Christ. _____
12. Manufacturing developed quickly in the United States. _____
13. Cotton was grown in the South. _____
14. The ice melted slowly. _____
15. We joined this great Church at the moment of our baptism. _____
16. The disciples chose seven men as deacons. _____
17. Experience develops character. _____
18. The ball was kicked out of the field. _____
19. After the Rosary, the children went to bed. _____
20. Paul hastened away. _____

Saint Thomas More, Pray for us!   J.M.J.   English 8 for Young Catholics   91

Lesson 48: VERBS

Kinds of Verbs According to Use: Being Verbs (Linking Verbs)

A verb that **expresses being or state of being** states a **condition** rather than an action.

Any form of the verb **be** expresses being.

Any verb that **may be replaced by a form of the verb** *be* **expresses state of being**. Such verbs include *appear, become, feel, grow, look, remain, seem, smell, sound,* and *taste*.

Being
The visitor **was** he.
Six brothers **were** his hosts.
The weather **had been** stormy.

State of Being
He **appeared** tired.
They **felt** happy.
They **remained** friends.

The verb *be* in its various forms is a **linking verb**.
A verb that may be replaced by a form of the verb *be* is a **linking verb**.
A noun, a pronoun, or an adjective that follows a linking verb refers to the subject.
A noun, a pronoun, or an adjective that follows a linking verb is a **subjective complement**.

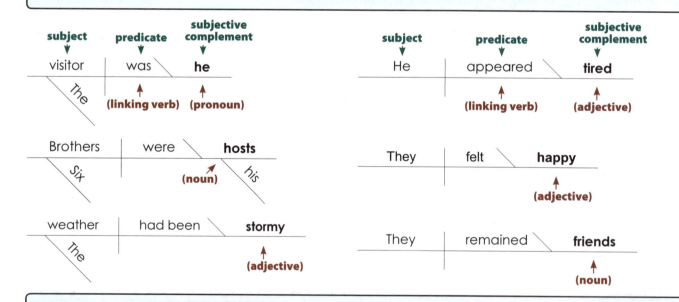

If a verb **cannot be replaced by** a form of the verb *be*, then that verb is **not a linking verb**.

Our Lady **appeared** to Bernadette.
Our Lord **felt** the blind man's eyes.
Only the woman **remained**.

VERBS

Lesson 48

Exercise 48A: Circle the linking verb in each sentence. Write S above each subject and SC above each subjective complement.

1. Simeon was a respected prophet.
2. This prophet was well-known throughout Judea.
3. Faith, hope, and charity are the theological virtues.
4. Of these, the greatest virtue is charity.
5. The rich young man felt very virtuous.
6. The Church has remained faithful to Jesus throughout the centuries.
7. None can remain indifferent to Christ's teaching.
8. St. Gregory's mother was St. Silvia.
9. The monastery at Monte Cassino became the home of many monks.
10. St. Benedict became their leader.

Exercise 48B: Diagram the following sentences.

1. Trees grow tall in fertile soil.

2. The family seemed tired after their long trip.

3. Saul, a persecutor of Christians, became Paul after his conversion.

Lesson 49 — VERBS

Qualities of Verbs: Voice

> A **verb** is the **part of speech** that expresses action, being, or state of being.
>
> In a **sentence**, the verb is a **predicate**. Its **function** is to make a statement about the subject. As a **predicate**, a verb has the qualities of **voice**, **tense**, **mood**, **person**, and **number**.

> **Voice** is the quality of a predicate that shows the **subject** as either the *doer* or the *receiver* of an action.
>
> A **predicate in the active voice** shows the **subject** as the *doer* of the action.
>
> A **predicate in the passive voice** shows the **subject** as the *receiver* of the action.

> **Predicates in the passive voice** are always **verb phrases**.
>
> They are made up of a **helping verb followed by a past participle** as the main verb.
>
> Helping verbs include *am, is, are, were, was, will be,* and *have been*.

Active Voice

    (subject)
    (doer) (predicate)
    ▼   ▼

The <u>pope</u> **prayed** the Rosary.
Those <u>adults</u> **will become** catechumens.
<u>God</u> **created** the world from nothing.
Our <u>pastor</u> **baptized** three babies.

Passive Voice

    (subject)
    (receiver) (predicate)
    ▼   ▼

The <u>Rosary</u> **was prayed** by the pope.
<u>They</u> **will be given** some study guides.
The <u>world</u> **was created** from nothing by God.
Three <u>babies</u> **were baptized** by our pastor.

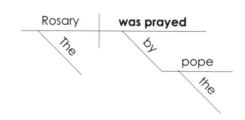

VERBS

Lesson 49

Exercise 49A: Rewrite the following sentences on the blank lines by changing the active to passive voice and the passive to active voice.

1. The poor people of Calcutta were helped by Mother Teresa.

2. Gold, frankincense, and myrrh were laid near the manger by the Magi.

3. In Denver, Dr. Clark met the Holy Father.

4. St. Patrick was taken to Ireland by slave traders.

5. The water was turned into wine by Jesus at the wedding of Cana.

6. Jesus washed the feet of His apostles.

7. Jesus raised Lazarus from the dead.

8. Pope Benedict XVI succeeded Pope John Paul II.

Exercise 49B: Diagram the following sentences:

1. The path to Heaven is shown to the faithful by the Church.

2. The Church shows the faithful the path to Heaven.

Lesson 50

VERBS

Qualities of Verbs: Tense: Simple Tenses

> The **tense** of a predicate tells the **time** of the action or the condition that is expressed.
> The **simple tenses** are the *present*, *past*, and *future*.
> The **form** of most verbs in the present tense changes in the past tense and in the passive voice.

Simple Tenses

Present tense   expresses an action or condition that is *current*, *habitual*, or *usual*
Past tense   expresses an action or condition that occurred *in the past*
Future tense   expresses an action or condition that will occur *in the future*
                The future tense requires the verb *shall* or *will* before the main verb.

The verb *write* in the simple tenses

	Active Voice	**Passive Voice**
Present	Frank and Mary frequently **write** letters.	Letters frequently **are written** by Frank and Mary.
Past	Paul **wrote** his epistles as he travelled.	Epistles **were written** by Paul as he travelled.
Future	Students **will write** thank you cards.	Thank you cards **will be written** by students.

Exercise 50A: Circle the predicate(s) in each sentence. Write the tense on the lines to the right.

1. Emperor Valerian superstitiously feared the Christians.   _____
2. He intensifies the persecution of Christians.   _____
3. In 257, Sixtus II was elected pope.   _____
4. The consecration of Sixtus as pope will be held in secret.   _____
5. A year later, Valerian enacted a harsher law.   _____
6. The prayers of the Mass are spoken in a quiet but firm voice.   _____
7. The people forgot the anger of those around them.   _____
8. Soon they will hear a crash at the door.   _____
9. "Give me your leaders, or we will kill you all." _____   _____
10. Sixtus and his four deacons stepped forward.   _____
11. They were killed on the spot and will join
     God in Heaven as martyrs.   _____   _____

VERBS

Lesson 50

Exercise 50B: Circle the correct predicate in the parentheses. On the lines to the right, write the tense (present, past, or future).

1. People often (use, used) incorrect English these days. _____

2. When we are adults, we children (spoke, will speak) English correctly. _____

3. I (learn, learned) several vocabulary words every week now. _____

4. We (look, looked) up new words when we run across them in a book. _____

5. The church (was built, will be built) during the reign of Charlemagne. _____

6. Next June, we (had, will have) a special Mass for our graduation. _____

7. Earlier, we (have, had) the flag-raising ceremony. _____

8. The letters (are written, were written) before we left for vacation. _____

9. The apostles (understand, understood) some of the parables. _____

10. God (says, said), "Let there be light," and there was light. _____

Exercise 50C: Fill in the blank with the correct form of the verb on the left. On the line to the right, write the tense of the predicate.

1. run   Yesterday morning, we _____ three miles. _____

2. catch   Last week, Dad _____ seven trout, which we ate. _____

3. go   We _____ swimming whenever it is sunny. _____

4. raise   The club _____ its membership fee again last month. _____

5. read   I _____ six books next summer. _____

6. choose   The books were _____ with care. _____

7. lead   The choir will be _____ by Susan again next year. _____

8. ring   Please _____ the bell. _____

9. keep   Will we _____ all the prayer books together? _____

10. speak   No words were _____ as the pope passed by. _____

Lesson 51: VERBS

Qualities of Verbs: Tense: Perfect Tenses

> The **tense** of the predicate tells the **time** of the action or the condition that is expressed.
> The **perfect tenses** are the *present perfect*, *past perfect*, and *future perfect*.
> **Perfect tenses** are distinguished by the use of a **past participle** and a **form of the helping verb** *have*.
> The **form** of verbs in the present tense changes in the perfect tenses.

Perfect Tenses

Present perfect tense   expresses an action or condition that
   a) happened at some indefinite time; or
   b) started in the past and continues into the present time.
To form the present perfect tense, use the helping verb *have* or *has* with the past participle.

Past perfect tense   expresses an action or condition that was completed before another past action started.
To form the past prefect tense, use the helping verb *had* with the past participle.

Future perfect tense   expresses an action or condition that will be completed before some specified time in the future.
To form the future perfect tense, use the helping verb *will have* with the past participle.

The verb *write* in the perfect tenses

	Active Voice	**Passive Voice**
Present Perfect	Frank **has written** some letters.	Some letters **have been written** by Frank.
Past Perfect	Paul **had written** an epistle before he left Rome.	An epistle **had been written** by Paul.
Future Perfect	They **will have written** thank you notes by July.	Thank you notes **will have been written**.

Exercise 51A: Circle the predicates that are in the perfect tenses. On the lines to the right, write whether they are in the present perfect, the past perfect, or the future perfect tense.

1. These parents have prepared their children well for Confirmation.   _____

2. The Holy Father will have finished the encyclical by Friday.   _____

3. Mark had written Peter's talks on Our Lord's life.   _____

4. Any tree that has not produced good fruit will be cut down.   _____

5. I have kept all these Commandments.   _____

6. Jesus had finished all He wanted to say.   _____

7. Six inches of snow will have fallen by dawn.   _____

VERBS

Lesson 51

Exercise 51B: Write the perfect tenses of the following verbs. Be sure to use the helping verbs that agree with the specified pronoun.

	Present Perfect	Past Perfect	Future Perfect
Example: I laugh	I have laughed	I had laughed	I will have laughed
1. you throw			
2. they forget			
3. it sinks			
4. we ride			
5. he shakes			
6. you lay			
7. she leads			

Exercise 51C: Write the verb in parentheses in the tense indicated.

A. Present Perfect **B.** Past Perfect **C.** Future Perfect

B 1. Diocletian (use) violence and bloodshed to attain his power. _____

C 2. Jesus (forgive) you by the time you leave the church. _____

A 3. We (learn) that our bodies are temples of the Holy Spirit. _____

B 4. Mark (convert) by Peter before he accompanied him to Rome. _____

C 5. We (know) them by their fruit. _____

C 6. Before the day is over, they (nail) Him to the Cross. _____

B 7. The men who (arrest) Jesus led Him off to the house of Caiphas. _____

C 8. We (finish) our lessons before dinner. _____

A 9. I (teach) in the Temple day after day. _____

A 10. They (crucify) Him, but He will rise from the dead. _____

Lesson 52

VERBS

Qualities of Verbs: Mood

> **Mood** is the quality of a verb that tells the **manner** in which the action or the condition is expressed.
>
> Two verb moods are the **indicative** and the **imperative**.

The Indicative Mood

> The **indicative mood** states a fact, denies a fact, or asks a question.
> *The pope is head of the Church.*   *Deacons may not say Mass.*   *Who will be the next pope?*
>
> The **progressive form of the indicative mood** denotes an action or condition that is going on or in progress.
> *It is raining in California today.*   *We have been planning a trip.*   *You will have been jogging.*
>
> The **emphatic form of the indicative mood** gives emphasis to the verb by placing the correct form of the verb *do* before the verb.
> *The choir does sing every Sunday.*   *Explorers did face dangers.*   *I did have breakfast.*
>
> The **potential form of the indicative mood** expresses permission, possibility, ability, necessity, or obligation. The helping verbs *may, might, can, could, must, should,* and *would* in front of the verb indicate the potential form.
> *You may go to the mall.*   *It might not have been difficult.*   *We can build a tree house.*
> *We must remain vigilant.*   *They should have taken a cab.*   *We would have arrived by then.*

The Imperative Mood

> The **imperative mood** gives a firm or mild command, or makes a request.
> *Sit, Rover!*   *Hang those clothes in your closet.*   *Pray for my aunt who is ill.*

VERBS

Lesson 53

The Indicative Mood

> The **indicative mood**
> – states a fact, denies a fact, or asks a question,
> – may be used in all six tenses, and
> – may be used in the active voice and in the passive voice.

States a fact	Our family usually attends the nine o'clock Mass on Sunday.
Denies a fact	Max did not drive himself to church today.
Asks a question	Where will we sit during Mass?

Tense	Active Voice	Passive Voice
Present	Roger **leads** the Rosary.	Prayers for the family **are requested**.
Past Tense	Jesus **prayed** over the dead girl.	A loud cry **was heard**.
Future Tense	Sandra **will babysit** tomorrow.	The benefit **will be held** over the weekend.
Present Perfect	Paula **has planned** her wedding.	The invitations **have been sent**.
Past Perfect	We **had jogged** before dinner.	The salads **had been prepared**.
Future Perfect	Marsha **will have graduated** by then.	Speeches **will have been given**.

Exercise 53: On the lines to the right, write the correct form of the verb in parentheses in the tense and voice indicated on the left.

Tense	Voice		
Present	Active	1.	Mark (do) his homework at his desk. _____
Future Perf.	Passive	2.	Greece (conquer). _____
Past	Active	3.	Jesus (weep) over Jerusalem. _____
Present Perf.	Passive	4.	A place (prepare) for us in Heaven. _____
Future	Active	5.	The Spirit of your Father (speak) in you. _____
Past Perfect	Passive	6.	The multitude (feed). _____
Past	Passive	7.	Constantine eventually (baptize). _____
Past	Active	8.	He (prefer) persuasion over force. _____
Future	Passive	9.	Whatever you bind on earth (bind) in Heaven. _____
Present Perf.	Active	10.	Our guardian angel (protect) us daily. _____

Lesson 54

VERBS

The Indicative Mood: Emphatic, Potential, and Progressive

Forms of the Indicative Mood

Form	Purpose	Helping Verbs	Tenses	Voice
Emphatic	Emphasizes the verb	*do, does, did*	Present and past	Active
Potential	Expresses permission, possibility, ability, necessity, or obligation	*may, might, can, could, must, should,* and *would*	All the tenses except the future tenses	Active and passive
Progressive	Expresses an action that is ongoing or in progress	Forms of the verb *be*	All six tenses	Active and passive

Emphatic Form
I **do like** your new haircut!
We **did enjoy** last week's ball game.

NOTE: The emphatic form does not apply to questions or negative statements.
Do you like your new haircut?
Harry and James do not enjoy baseball.

Potential Form
Permission — You **may leave** now, Mary.
Possibility — Mother **may** (or **might**) **have allowed** you to stay.
Ability — My little brother **can** (or **could**) **count** to ten.
Necessity — You **must make** a firm decision.
Obligation — We **should pay** our dues as soon as we can.

Progressive Form
The Flanagans **are enjoying** their tour of the Holy Land.
The pilot **will have been flying** on a full tank of gas.
The letters **were being written** from camp.

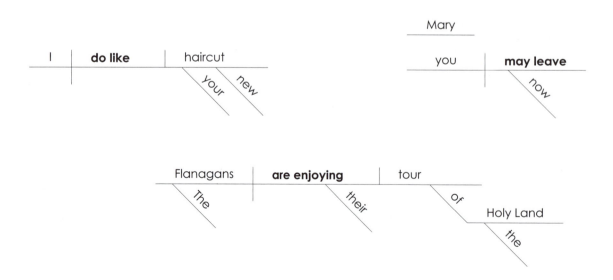

102   English 8 for Young Catholics   J.M.J.   *Saint Thomas More, Pray for us!*

VERBS

Lesson 54

Exercise 54: Above each verb phrase in italics, write A for active voice or P for passive voice. On the lines to the right, write Emphatic, Potential, or Progressive to indicate the form of the indicative mood of the verb phrase.

                A
Example: I *must arrive* earlier next time.   Potential

1. Mother *did send* me to the store. _____

2. I *should respond* wholeheartedly to my vocation. _____

3. My family *does pray* the daily Rosary. _____

4. Christ *did come* to save all men. _____

5. He *should have been welcomed* by us. _____

6. My sister *will be joining* the Carmelites in the fall. _____

7. I *can offer* this up for the poor souls in Purgatory. _____

8. The Christians of Damascus *were being pursued* by Paul. _____

9. Saul *did fall* from his horse upon seeing Christ. _____

10. Christ *could have avoided* death if He had wanted to. _____

11. The apostles *should have prayed* with Jesus in the garden. _____

12. Each one of us *is being asked* by the Church to spread the Gospel. _____

13. I *must follow* my conscience. _____

14. Confessions *should have been scheduled* for today. _____

15. She *will have been speaking* by the time we arrive. _____

16. They *do participate* in the March for Life every year. _____

17. He *might have been left* behind, but he made it somehow. _____

18. The souls in Purgatory *are being purified* so they may enter Heaven. _____

19. Father, *could* you *hear* my confession after Mass today? _____

20. Charles *has been going* to camp all week. _____

Lesson 55: VERBS

The Imperative Mood

> The **imperative mood**
> – gives a firm or mild command, or makes a request,
> – is always in the present tense, and
> – has "you" as the subject.
>
> When a predicate is in the imperative mood, the subject is understood, that is, it is not expressed.

Firm Command   Stand, everyone!
Mild Command   Drive carefully through this intersection.
Request   Have mercy on me, a sinner, O Lord.

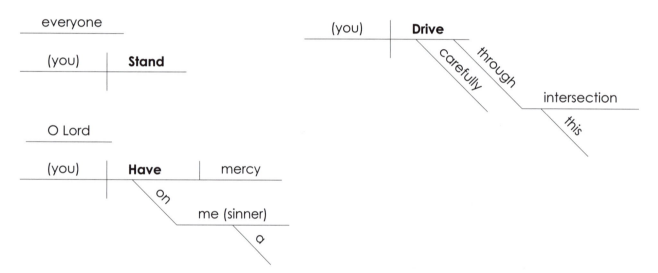

Exercise 55: Circle the predicates that are in the imperative mood.

1. Be perfect as your heavenly Father is perfect.
2. Father, glorify Your Son, so that Your Son may glorify You.
3. Love one another as I have loved you.
4. Keep those You have given Me true to Your name.
5. Go forth and preach to all nations; tell them the good news of salvation.
6. Consider the lilies of the field; they do not worry about what they shall wear.
7. Keep your voices down, children, and listen carefully.

VERBS

Lesson 56

Qualities of Verbs: Person and Number

> A **predicate** must **always agree with its subject or subjects in person and number**. Except for the verb *be*, the **form** of the verb changes only when the predicate is in the third person, singular number, present tense.
> In a **verb phrase**, only the **helping verb changes**. The main verb remains the same.

Person	Singular	Plural	Singular	Plural
	Active Voice		Passive Voice	
First	I choose	We choose	I am chosen	We are chosen
Second	You choose	You choose	You are chosen	You are chosen
Third	He/she/it chooses	They choose	He/she/it is chosen	They are chosen

Exercise 56: Underline the subject(s) and circle the predicate in each sentence. On the lines to the right, write the person and number of each predicate.

Example: <u>Frank</u> and <u>Mary</u> (have sung) in the choir all year.   3rd, plural

1. My vocation is a special and unique gift from God.

2. Pope John Paul II has named twenty-two new cardinals.

3. Two prelates are "cardinals *in pectore*."

4. Their names will remain secret for now.

5. Your group and ours must speak out for the protection of all human life.

6. Food and other supplies were assembled at the Knights of Columbus halls.

7. People have been sharing their food, water, and homes.

8. Our pastor and the mayor are amazed at the unity of this community.

9. Everyone is now safe.

10. None are missing.

11. Water, food, and clothing have been distributed to each family.

12. The storm will pass, and they will rebuild. _____

Lesson 57: VERBS

Subject / Predicate Agreement: Person and Number

A **predicate** must always **agree with its subject in person and number**. In some sentences, the subject is not quickly identified.

When a sentence begins with "**There**" or "**Here**," the subject follows the predicate.

Sometimes a **parenthetical expression** is located between the subject and the predicate in a sentence. A **parenthetical expression** is a word or phrase that is inserted into a sentence to add explanation. Sometimes a **parenthetical expression** is located before the subject in a sentence.

In each instance, the predicate must always agree with the subject in person and number.

There **are** <u>medals</u> in the display case.

Here **comes** the troop <u>leader</u>.

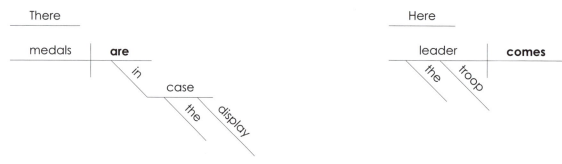

<u>James</u>, *in addition to his sisters*, **practices** piano two hours every day.
The <u>lessons</u> *in this saint's story* **impress** most readers.
In any emergency, <u>we</u> **keep** our minds alert.
As for the history of the shrine, here **are** some <u>leaflets</u> for your information.

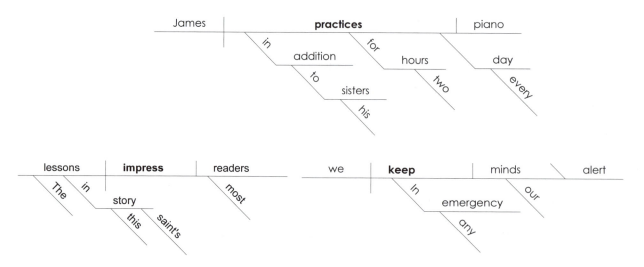

106 English 8 for Young Catholics   J.M.J.   *Saint Thomas More, Pray for us!*

VERBS

Lesson 57

Exercise 57A: Circle the correct predicate in each sentence.

1. Some people (says, say) the March for Life, the annual pro-life demonstration, (is, are) one of the longest continuous protests in U.S. history.

2. The March (has, have) had its memorable moments.

3. The very first March, January 22, 1974, (remains, remain) etched in the memory of Nellie Gray.

4. Picture it. She (is, are) the group's founder and president.

5. At twelve o'clock on that day, there (is, are) no one on the steps of the Capitol.

6. Suddenly, the buses (starts, start) rolling up.

7. Officials (has, have) estimated 20,000 demonstrators were present.

8. We (has, have) to try to reach one person at a time.

Exercise 57B: On the lines to the right, write the correct form of the verb in parentheses. All sentences are in the present tense.

1. Christ's example of self-giving and sacrifice (serve) as our perfect model. _____

2. If you need more milk, there (be) some in the refrigerator. _____

3. Your booklet, in addition to these, (suffice) for our small group. _____

4. In the closet, there (be) additional folding chairs. _____

5. Each Mass, above other things, (be) a sacrifice. _____

6. The priest, during Lent, (wear) purple. _____

7. Here (be) some candles for the vigil. _____

8. How (do) Christians prepare for Easter? _____

9. Here (be) a few ideas. _____

10. We need more communion wafers. There (be) some in the sacristy. _____

11. Sundays of every week (be) considered Holy Days of Obligation. _____

12. On these days, every Christian (participate) at Mass. _____

VERBS

Subject / Predicate Agreement: Compound Subjects Connected by *And*

> **Compound subjects connected by** *and* **require a singular predicate** when the subjects are the same person or thing.
> **Compound subjects connected by** *and* **require a plural predicate** when the subjects are separate persons or things.

Compound subjects are the same person My friend and pen pal **writes** me every Memorial Day.
Our coach and pastor **helps** us in many ways.

Compound subjects are separate persons My friend and his brother **are** altar boys.
St. Peter and St. Paul **were** great leaders of the Church.

Exercise 58: Circle the correct predicate in each sentence.

1. Ontario and New York (has, have) shrines dedicated to St. Isaac Jogues.
2. Our Savior and Redeemer always (forgives, forgive) us when we are sorry.
3. Saints Cyril and Methodius (was, were) consecrated bishops by Pope Adrian II.
4. Holy water and crucifixes (is, are) sacramentals which give us actual grace.
5. Our Queen and Mother (shows, show) us the way to Christ.
6. The president and owner of the company (lets, let) his employees off for Good Friday.
7. The marcher and supporter of life (was, were) not stopped by the snowstorm or the cold.
8. Confessors and moral theologians (shares, share) the same patron, St. Alphonsus Liguori.
9. The founder and leader of the Jesuits (was, were) determined to obey the pope.
10. The secretary and interpreter for Peter (was, were) converted by him.
11. The mother and father of the baby (takes, take) him to the church to be baptized.
12. The father and provider (attends, attend) daily Mass with his family.
13. The brother and sister (learns, learn) to be patient with each other.
14. The angels and saints (is, are) praying for us from Heaven.
15. The virgin and martyr (was, were) killed by a Roman soldier.

VERBS

Lesson 59

Subject / Predicate Agreement: Compound Subjects Preceded by *Each, Every, Many A,* or *No*

> **Singular compound subjects** that are connected by *and* but **preceded by** *each*, *every*, *many a*, or *no* require a singular predicate.

Each parent <u>and</u> grandparent **plans** to attend the Confirmation.
Every boy <u>and</u> girl **has received** a holy card.
Many a Catholic man <u>and</u> woman **attends** daily Mass.
No faithful believer <u>and</u> disciple **goes** unrewarded.

Exercise 59: Circle the correct predicate in each sentence.

1. Many a man and woman (has, have) been converted by the presence of Christ in church.
2. Every boy and girl (looks, look) forward to Christmas.
3. No true disciple and follower of Jesus (is, are) ever without a cross.
4. Each sacrifice and act of penance done out of love (brings, bring) us true happiness.
5. Every challenge and test (brings, bring) us closer to God.
6. Many a boy and girl (is, are) called to the religious life.
7. (Is, Are) every boy and girl who is called generous enough to follow Him?
8. Many an elementary homeschooler and high school homeschooler (receives, receive) excellent grades.
9. Every candidate and aspirant to the religious life (spends, spend) time getting to know Christ better.
10. No prayer and petition to God (goes, go) unheeded.
11. Each portrait and painting of the saints (reminds, remind) us of how to follow Christ.
12. Every resolution and decision to follow Christ more closely (is, are) accompanied by His grace.
13. Many a path and road (leads, lead) to destruction, but there is only one that leads to Heaven.
14. Each and every predicate in a sentence (has, have) at least one subject.
15. No thought and action (is, are) unknown to God.

Lesson 60: VERBS

Subject / Predicate Agreement: Compound Subjects Preceded by *Neither / Nor* or *Either / Or*

> **Singular subjects** of the **same** person connected by *nor* or *or* require a **singular predicate**.
> **Plural subjects** of the **same** person connected by *nor* or *or* require a **plural predicate**.

Neither Michael *nor* Paul **is** able to attend.
Either my brothers *or* my sisters **go** instead.

> When two or more subjects of a **different** person or number are connected by *nor* or *or*, the predicate agrees in person and number with the subject that is nearest to it.

Neither Mom *nor* the twins **arrive** late for Dad's birthday party.
Neither the twins *nor* Mom **arrives** late for Dad's birthday party.

Either the governor's assistant *or* his secretaries **prepare** the menu.
Either the governor's secretaries *or* his assistant **prepares** the menu.

Exercise 60: Circle the correct predicate in each sentence.

1. Neither Spanish nor Latin (is, are) difficult for me.
2. Either my books or his book (was, were) returned to the library.
3. Neither Columbus nor his sailors (was, were) in the East Indies as they thought.
4. Either the cardinals or the bishops (was, were) to meet the Holy Father this month.
5. Neither the managers nor the employees (is, were) willing to work on Sunday.
6. Neither the Cuban people nor their leader (was, were) untouched by the pope's words.
7. Neither gold nor riches (leads, lead) a person down the path to Heaven.
8. Either sacrifice or self-denial done out of love (leads, lead) us to Christ.
9. Either the cookies or the pizza (has, have) upset my stomach.
10. Neither the pope nor the cardinals (has, have) any knowledge of who the next pope will be.

VERBS

Lesson 61

Subject / Predicate Agreement: Collective Noun Subjects

> A **collective noun subject** requires a **singular predicate** if the noun is considered to be **a single unit**.
>
> A **collective noun subject** requires a **plural predicate** if the noun is considered to be separate **individuals**.

A flock of sheep **was locked** in a pen.
A flock of sheep were eating their food.

This committee **represents** the city's poor.
The committee **are selected** for their areas of specialty.

Exercise 61: Circle the correct predicate in each sentence.

1. The altar boys' club (has, have) many exciting activities.
2. The bouquet of red and white roses (was, were) placed at the foot of the statue of Mary.
3. Our soccer team usually (wins, win) against that team.
4. Every spring and fall, the flock of geese (arrives, arrive) in our pond.
5. Our team (is, are) well prepared for the match.
6. The crowd (was, were) quiet during the pope's speech.
7. The orchestra (performs, perform) in the plaza once a year.
8. The seminarians' choir beautifully (sings, sing) the Gregorian Chant.
9. The audience (leaves, leave) their seats at the end of the concert.
10. The whole herd of cattle (was, were) bought by one rancher.
11. The choir (is, are) famous for the annual performance of Handel's *Messiah*.
12. The group of altar boys (was, were) divided on where to go for Independence Day.
13. This bunch of bananas (was, were) priced at sixty cents per pound.
14. The committee (submits, submit) the annual budget in October of every year.
15. The team (has, have) received the highest ranking in the state again this year.

Lesson 62: VERBS

Words Used as Verbs and Nouns

> Some words may be either of two *parts of speech*, **verbs** or **nouns**.
>
> A word is a **verb** if it **expresses** *action, being,* or *state of being*.
> In a sentence, a **verb functions** as a predicate and it makes a statement about the subject.
>
> A word is a **noun** if it **names** *a person, a place* or *a thing*.
> In a sentence, a **noun** may **function** as a *subject, subjective complement, apposition, direct address, exclamation, direct object, indirect object,* or *object of a preposition*.

Predicate   *Act* as a verb: Always **act** according to God's laws.
Subjective Complement *Act* as a noun: Sin is an **act** of disobedience to God.

Exercise 62: Write Noun or Verb for the part of speech of the italicized word in each sentence.

1. The *care* and respect of Mother Teresa toward the poor were obvious in the way she embraced them. _____
2. The *guard* on watch was afraid when he heard a loud noise. _____
3. The boys *crowd* into the elevator. _____
4. Father John and Father Mike *address* the parish council. _____
5. The *time* we spend in adoration before the Blessed Sacrament is well spent. _____
6. We *time* ourselves to see how long the memorization takes. _____
7. Homeschooling parents *watch* their children grow in wisdom and knowledge. _____
8. By my *watch*, it is seven. _____
9. The *crowd* seems larger in number. _____
10. The Sisters of Charity *care* for those who are sick and homeless. _____
11. The watch dogs *guard* the entrance to the warehouse. _____
12. The bulletin *states* that there will be extra time for Confession on Friday. _____
13. On the envelope, write your *address*. _____
14. Our guardian angels *envelop* us with their protection. _____

CHAPTER 5

ADVERBS

ADVERBS

ADVERBS

Chapter Outline

CHAPTER FIVE

I. **Kinds of adverbs**
   A. Adverbs of time
   B. Adverbs of place
   C. Adverbs of manner
   D. Adverbs of degree
   E. Adverbs of affirmation and of negation
   F. Interrogative adverbs
   G. Adverbial objectives

II. **Degrees of comparison of adverbs**

III. **Adverbs and adjectives**
   A. Correct use in sentences
   B. Correct use after linking verbs

IV. **Correct use of** *farther*, *further*, **and** *equally*

Lesson 63: ADVERBS

Adverbs

> An **adverb** is the part of speech that denotes time, place, manner, degree, or affirmation or negation.
> An **adverb may modify** a <u>verb</u>, an <u>adjective</u>, or <u>another adverb</u>.
> An **adverb may never modify** a <u>noun</u>.

Most adverbs modify verbs.

Mary Magdalen <u>went</u> **early** to the tomb.
The rich young man <u>walked</u> **away**.
Zachaeus <u>climbed</u> **high** in the tree in order to see Our Lord.
Jesus <u>walked</u> **slowly** as He carried His cross.
Indeed, Peter <u>was walking</u> on the water.

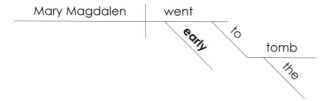

Some adverbs modify adjectives.

Unbearably <u>sad</u>, the rich young man walked away.
Zachaeus was **unusually** <u>short</u>.
Peter became **greatly** <u>terrified</u>.

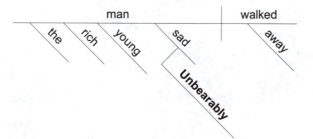

Some adverbs modify other adverbs.

Somewhat <u>impetuously</u>, Peter approached Our Lord.
Mary Magdalen approached the tomb **rather** <u>anxiously</u>.
The young man **very** <u>slowly</u> turned away.

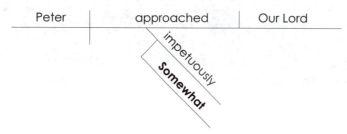

ADVERBS

Lesson 64

Adverbs of Time, Place, Manner, and Degree

An **adverb of time** answers the question *when?* or *how often?* It usually modifies a verb.

Some Adverbs of Time

again	early	frequently	now	seldom	then
already	ever	immediately	often	sometimes	today
always	finally	later	once	soon	tomorrow
before	first	never	recently	still	usually

An **adverb of place** answers the question *where?* It usually modifies a verb.

Some Adverbs of Place

above	below	forth	inside	under	
away	down	forward	out	up	
back	everywhere	here	outside	within	
behind	far	in	there		

An **adverb of manner** answers the question *how?* or *in what manner?* It usually modifies a verb.

Adverbs of **manner** are usually formed by adding **ly** or **ily** to adjectives. There are exceptions.

Some Adverbs of Manner

Some Exceptions

badly	carefully	angrily	fast
clearly	cheerfully	easily	hard
eagerly	gleefully	mightily	well

An **adverb of degree** answers the question *how much?* or *how little?* It may modify a verb, an adjective, or another adverb.

Some Adverbs of Degree

almost	greatly	much	really	too
barely	hardly	partly	scarcely	very
extremely	little	quite	sufficiently	
fully	merely	rather	unusually	

Saint Thomas More, Pray for us!   J.M.J.   *English 8 for Young Catholics*

Lesson 64: ADVERBS

Exercise 64A: Circle the adverb(s) in each sentence.

1. Make use of the confessional **frequently**.
2. Robert understood the lesson **very quickly**.
3. James fixed his gaze **upward** on the crucifix.
4. Her cousins **truly** think Carol is **unusually** tall.
5. I can **barely** hear you.
6. Christ preached **there authoritatively**.
7. Cars **always** travel **too fast** on this curvy road.
8. I **merely** told them the truth.
9. The weather **suddenly** turned **extremely** cold.
10. **Inside**, it was **mercifully** warm.
11. God **readily** forgives repentant sinners.
12. Paul arrived **promptly** for the novena.
13. With a light heart, the centurion **gratefully** returned to his home.
14. **Majestically**, the victorious king went **back** to his castle.
15. Martha put her books **aside**.

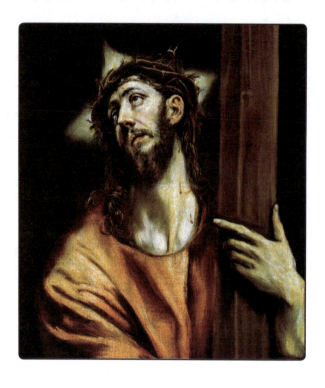

Exercise 64B: Diagram the following sentences.

1. In the end, the particularly conscientious student very quietly puts his books away.

2. Invariably, Father Andre's encouraging words gently comfort the sick.

ADVERBS

Lesson 65

Adverbs of Affirmation and of Negation

> An **adverb of affirmation** or **of negation** tells whether a statement is *true* or *false*.
> An adverb of **affirmation** affirms; an adverb of **negation** denies.

Adverbs of Affirmation
indeed
undoubtedly
yes

Adverbs of Negation
no
not
never*

*The word *never* may function as either an adverb of negation of an adverb of time.

Indeed, Peter was walking on the water.
The Pharisees **undoubtedly** were mystified by Christ's predictions.
Yes, our team will compete in the tournament.
I will **not** take French this year.
Never again will I eat three pieces of chocolate cheese cake after a big meal!

> If a sentence has one negative word, such as *not*, avoid using another negative word, such as *no*, *no one*, or *never*.
> Instead, use a word such as *any*, *anyone* or *ever*.

We do **not** want **any** dessert.   We do **not** see **anyone** we know.

Exercise 65: On the lines to the right, write *no, no one* or *never,* or *any, anyone,* or *ever*.

1. I do not have _____ extra staples.   _____
2. Of the whole group, there was _____ who knew Dr. Sawyer.   _____
3. Have you not _____ visited Washington, D.C.?   _____
4. Hasn't _____ found my ballpoint pen yet?   _____
5. There were not _____ onions on the pizza.   _____
6. Don't you have _____ extra change in your pocket?   _____
7. _____ take the Lord's name in vain.   _____
8. The girls have all the choir books; there aren't _____ left for us.   _____

Saint Thomas More, Pray for us!   J.M.J.   English 8 for Young Catholics   119

Lesson 66: ADVERBS

Interrogative Adverbs

> An **interrogative adverb** asks a question.
> The **interrogative adverbs** are *how? when? where?* and *why?*

How do they care so well for their flock?
When did Jesus perform His first miracle?
Where will Dan go later this morning?
Why should we often pray to the saints?

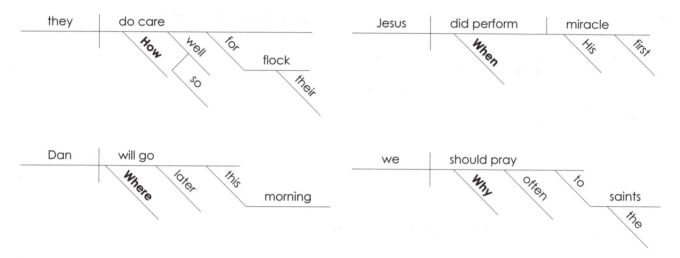

Exercise 66: Fill in the blank with the appropriate interrogative adverb.

1. Judas, _____ will we know He is Jesus whom we must arrest?

2. _____ is Bethlehem located?

3. _____ is the Holy Hour at the church?

4. _____ did God make us?

5. _____ is All Souls' Day?

6. They asked, "_____ often must we forgive another?"

7. Mary asked the angel, "_____ can this be?"

ADVERBS

Lesson 67

Adverbial Objectives

> An **adverbial objective** is a noun that performs the function of an adverb.
> An **adverbial objective** expresses time, distance, measure, weight, value, or direction.

The trip took three **hours**.
My house is located one **mile** away.
The new baby weighs eight **pounds**.
Those scarves cost six **dollars**.
Our house is that **way**.

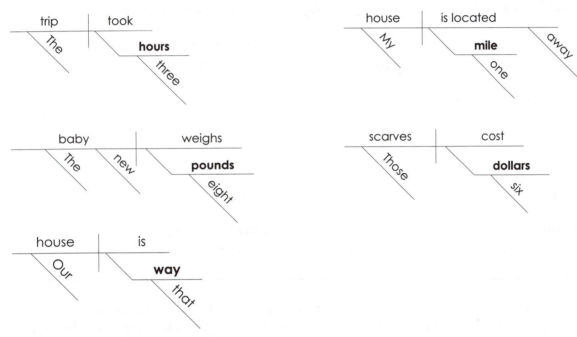

Exercise 67: Complete each sentence with an adverbial objective expressing the quality in parentheses.

(weight)   1. Our new brother weighs only seven _____.

(measure)   2. The tree in our back yard is now eighteen _____ tall.

(value)   3. The catechism costs ten _____.

(time)   4. Mary and her family left for Ireland two _____ ago.

(measure)   5. Our Lady's statue is approximately seven _____ tall.

(direction) 6. Turn your head that _____ to see the famous shrine.

(weight)   7. I felt one hundred _____ lighter after Confession.

(time)   8. The priest who came from Rome arrived this _____.

Saint Thomas More, Pray for us! — J.M.J. — English 8 for Young Catholics

Lesson 68: ADVERBS

Degrees of Comparison of Adverbs

Adverbs may be used to express **degrees of comparison** of quality.
Most adverbs express three degrees of comparison: **positive**, **comparative**, and **superlative**.

The **positive** degree
— is the adverb itself,
— shows quality,
— shows no comparison, and
— is the basis for forming the comparative and superlative degrees of comparison.

Max runs **fast**.   (The quality is not compared with any other.)

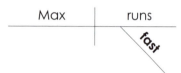

The **comparative** degree shows quality in **greater or lesser degree**.

Max runs **faster** than Philip.
(The quality is compared in a greater degree.)

Dave runs **less fast** than Philip.
(The quality is compared in a lesser degree.)

The **superlative** degree shows quality in the **greatest or least degree**.

Of the entire track team, Bob runs the **fastest**.
(The quality is compared in the greatest degree.)

Sam runs the **least fast** of the track team members.
(The quality is compared in the least degree.)

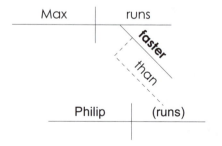

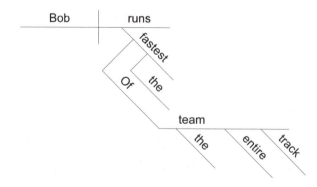

122 English 8 for Young Catholics

ADVERBS

Lesson 68

Rules for Forming the Degrees of Comparison of Adverbs

Some **adverbs** form the **comparative** degree by adding *er* to the positive degree; they form the **superlative** degree by adding *est* to the positive degree.

Positive	Comparative	Superlative
soon	sooner	soonest
hard	harder	hardest
late	later	latest

Adverbs that end in *ly* usually form the comparative degree by adding **more** or **less** to the positive degree. They form the superlative degree by adding **most** or **least** to the positive degree.

Positive	Comparative	Superlative
securely	more/less securely	most/least securely
timidly	more/less timidly	most/least timidly
gracefully	more/less gracefully	most/least gracefully

Some adverbs have irregular comparisons. Each one is different, so it is necessary to learn their comparative and superlative degrees.

Positive	Comparative	Superlative
badly	worse	worst
far	farther	farthest
little	less	least
much	more	most
well	better	best

Some adverbs do not have degrees of comparison.
  a. Some adverbs of time and place:
     above, again, always, down, here, immediately, now, then, when, where
  b. Some adverbs express completeness and cannot be compared:
     absolutely, continually, entirely, eternally, exactly, forever, fully, immediately, infinitely, never, perfectly, truly, universally

Lesson 68: ADVERBS

Exercise 68: Write the comparative degree and the superlative degree of each adverb. If no comparison applies, write NONE.

Positive	Comparative	Superlative
Example: slowly	more/less slowly	most/least slowly
1. quickly		
2.	less	
3.		most/least foolishly
4. late		
5. well		
6.	more/less loudly	
7. perfectly		
8.		soonest
9.	more	
10.		most/least courteously
11. immediately		
12. fast		
13.	more/less often	
14. badly		
15. readily		
16.		most/least eagerly
17.	higher	
18. always		
19.		farthest
20.		safest

ADVERBS

Lesson 69

Correct Use of Adverbs and Adjectives in Sentences

> An **adverb** modifies a verb, an adjective, or another adverb.
> An **adjective** modifies a noun or a pronoun.

      adjectives **noun** **verb** **adverb**   **verb**   **adverb**
The **blind** man shouted **loudly**, and Jesus heard him **clearly**.

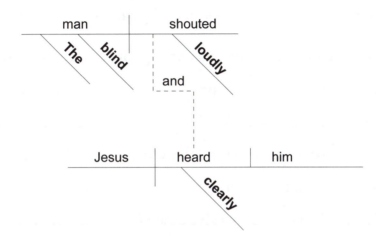

    adjectives   **noun** **adverb** **verb** **adjectives** **noun**
The **dog's loud**, **clear** bark **abruptly** woke me from **a deep** sleep.

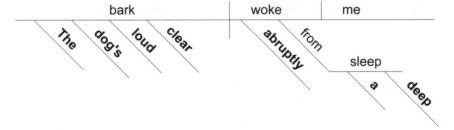

Exercise 69A: Circle the correct adjective or adverb in parentheses. Underline the word it modifies.

1. James studies very (serious, seriously) before he has an important test.
2. Even in this large auditorium, her (quiet, quietly) voice carried well.
3. Mother (patient, patiently) taught us to say our prayers.
4. Her (sensible, sensibly) answer convinced the jury.
5. The new church was built (solid, solidly) of bricks and stone.
6. The baby is sleeping (comfortable, comfortably) in her crib.
7. The nun was dressed (simple, simply) in her habit.

Lesson 69: ADVERBS

Exercise 69B: Circle the adverbs and underline the descriptive adjectives in each sentence.

1. The young skater fell hard upon the hard ice, but he hardly felt it through his thick snowsuit.
2. Fran knew little about the cloistered nuns, but she cared enough to learn more details.
3. His last homily did not last long, but it definitely made a lasting impression.
4. Tommy could not be still through the entire movie, but he remembers it still.
5. "No," he vehemently said, "I will not ever deny You, Lord!"
6. Why does the slow snail slowly glide the width of the path to the long grass beyond?

Exercise 69C: Complete each sentence with an appropriate adverb or adjective.

1. Each nail was _____ hammered by the carpenter. _____
2. The organist played _____ at the Easter Vigil. _____
3. The missionary priest rode on a _____ mule into the wilderness. _____
4. The _____ smell of the roses filled the church. _____
5. We should listen _____ when our parents give us advice. _____
6. Every guest _____ enjoyed the party. _____

Exercise 69D: Diagram the following sentences.

1. This little saint, a powerful intercessor, is universally acclaimed.

2. Do not foolishly underestimate the strong, lasting power of persistent prayer.

ADVERBS

Lesson 70

Correct Use of Adverbs and Adjectives after Linking Verbs

> If some form of the verb **be** may replace the predicate in a sentence, then the predicate is a linking verb. The word following the predicate may be a noun, a pronoun or an **adjective**, but not an adverb.
>
> When an adjective follows a linking verb, it is a **subjective complement**, just as a noun or pronoun would be.

	(is)
Predicate is a linking verb	The attorney **looks** intent as he approaches the witness.
Predicate is an action verb	The attorney **looks** intently at the witness.
	(is)
Predicate is a linking verb	The judge **seems** stern.
Predicate is an action verb.	The judge **addresses** the attorney sternly.

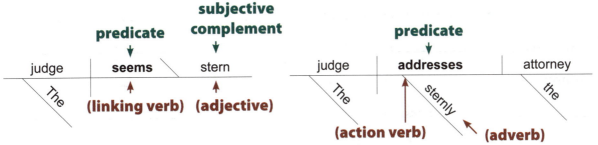

Exercise 70: Circle the correct word in parentheses in each sentence.

1. Chris felt (sad, sadly) that her bad cold prevented her from playing outdoors.
2. Francis dealt (merciful, mercifully) with the robbers who had beaten him.
3. Mrs. Thompson thinks (kind, kindly) of all her neighbors.
4. She is (charitable, charitably) toward them.
5. The children said Our Lady appeared (radiant, radiantly).
6. "Please remain (calm, calmly)," urged the castle guard.
7. Their nervousness lessened as they became more (certain, certainly) of their situation.
8. Your love and mercy will (sure, surely) carry me, O Lord.
9. My poor sister is tone deaf, and she sings (poor, poorly).
10. Please speak (soft, softly) to the baby.

Lesson 71

ADVERBS

Correct Use of *Farther, Further,* and *Equally*

> **Farther** refers to distance. **Further** denotes "in addition to."
> Both **farther** and **further** may be used as adverbs or as adjectives.

Adverb	We live **farther** from the lake than you do.
Adjective	The mountain is on the **farther** side of the state.
Adverb	I have nothing **further** to say.
Adjective	There were no **further** items on the agenda.

Exercise 71: Complete the sentence with *farther* or *further*.

1. Mark's house is _____ from here than mine.
2. Do you wish to carry this discussion _____?
3. Andrew went to college to pursue his education _____.
4. We took the boat to the _____ shore.
5. Constantinople is _____ east than I expected.
6. I have _____ need of your assistance.
7. What _____ need have we of witnesses?
8. Peter has read _____ into this book than I have.
9. We need not seek any _____ than Christ to find our purpose.
10. The pope has defined this matter; no _____ discussion is necessary.

> **Equally** means *as* when it modifies an adjective or an adverb.
> Never use *as* between *equally* and the adjective or the adverb.

Faith and works are **equally** important in the Christian life.
Matthew and Martha are **equally** anxious to learn.
These two books are **equally** informative.

CHAPTER 6

PREPOSITIONS, CONJUNCTIONS, INTERJECTIONS

PREPOSITIONS, CONJUNCTIONS, INTERJECTIONS

PREPOSITIONS, CONJUNCTIONS, INTERJECTIONS

Chapter Outline

CHAPTER SIX

I. **Prepositions – definition and function**
II. **Words used as prepositions and adverbs**
III. **Correct use of prepositions**
   A. *Between/among* and *beside/besides*
   B. *In/into* and *from/off*
   C. *Differ with/differ from* and *angry with/angry at*
IV. **Prepositional phrases**
   A. Adjectival
   B. Adverbial
V. **Conjunctions – definition and functions**
VI. **Kinds of conjunctions**
   A. Coordinate conjunctions
      1. Connect words and phrases
      2. Connect independent clauses
   B. Subordinate conjunctions (connect dependent clauses to independent clauses)
   C. Conjunctive adverbs
VII. **Correct use of *like/as* and *like/as if***
VIII. **Interjections**

Saint Thomas More, Pray for us!

Lesson 72: PREPOSITIONS, CONJUNCTIONS, INTERJECTIONS

Prepositions—Definition and Function

> A **preposition** is a part of speech. It is a word placed before a noun or pronoun to show its relationship to another word in the sentence.

> The **object of the preposition** is the noun or pronoun that follows a preposition. The preposition, its object, and any modifiers of the object form a **prepositional phrase**.

> A **prepositional phrase** may modify a noun, a pronoun, or a verb.

Most Common Prepositions

about	before	during	of	toward
above	behind	except	off	under
across	beside	for	on	until
after	besides	from	over	up
against	between	in	past	with
among	beyond	into	through	within
around	by	like	throughout	without
at	down	near	to	

Some Compound Prepositions

according to	apart from	because of	in front of	on account of
ahead of	as to	by means of	in spite of	on top of
along with	aside from	in addition to	instead of	owing to

Prepositional Phrase: <u>preposition</u>, object, and modifiers of the object

Is your mother **in** the chapel?

Go **into** the world and preach the Gospel.

In addition to St. Jane de Chantal, Mom told us **about** St. Joan.

They arrived **at** the Confirmation early **in spite of** the bad weather.

PREPOSITIONS, CONJUNCTIONS, INTERJECTIONS

Lesson 72

Diagrams help us to visualize the way prepositional phrases relate to other words in a sentence.

The Pharisees **in** the Temple **of** Jerusalem argued the Law **of** Moses **among** themselves **with** great intensity.

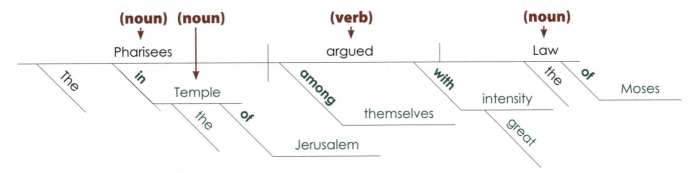

The priests **at** Lourdes blessed those **with** physical afflictions.

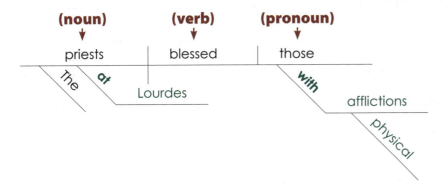

In addition **to** other groups **of** citizens, the members **of** the town council discussed **at** great length the ones **with** special needs.

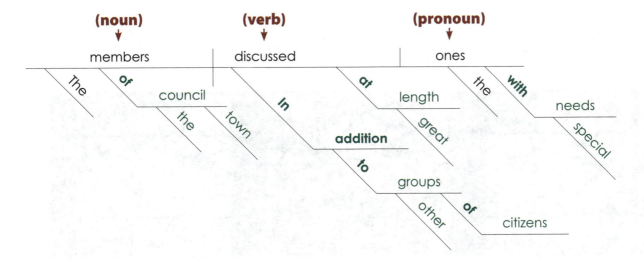

Saint Thomas More, Pray for us!   J.M.J.   English 8 for Young Catholics   133

Lesson 72: PREPOSITIONS, CONJUNCTIONS, INTERJECTIONS

Exercise 72A: Circle the prepositions in each sentence. On the lines, write NOUN, PRONOUN, or VERB for the part of speech the prepositional phrase modifies.

1. Having no choice, they sailed against the wind. _____
2. Mom served apple pie with ice cream. _____
3. Besides Frank, Harry was an altar server this morning. _____
4. Tom pulled the tablecloth from the table and the glass fell over. _____
5. I would like a box of chocolates, please. _____
6. Please place another pillow under his head. _____
7. The lady on the porch waved a fly away. _____
8. The books on this shelf will be read this summer. _____
9. Linda lagged behind because she carefully looked at all the artwork. _____
10. Christ is truly present in the Eucharist. _____
11. When we receive the Eucharist, we receive the Body of Christ. _____
12. To some people, this may seem impossible. _____
13. It is a doctrine of the Catholic Church. _____

Exercise 72B: Diagram the following sentence.

It is indeed a doctrine of the Church.

PREPOSITIONS, CONJUNCTIONS, INTERJECTIONS
Lesson 73

Words Used as Prepositions and Adverbs

> Some words may be used as prepositions and adverbs.
> In a sentence, a **preposition** is always followed by a noun or pronoun object.
> In a sentence, an **adverb** does not have an object.

Words That May Be Used as Prepositions and Adverbs

about	before	beyond	near	past	under
above	behind	by	off	through	within
after	besides	down	on	throughout	without
around	between	in	over	up	

Preposition   The priest knelt **before** the altar.
Adverb   Have you ever visited the National Shrine **before**?

Exercise 73: On the line, write whether the italicized word is a preposition or an adverb.

_____ 1. Christ fell *down* on His Way to Calvary.

_____ 2. The young boy walked *outside* and saw a blue jay.

_____ 3. Jesus was preaching *in* the temple.

_____ 4. He looked *about* and saw some puzzled faces.

_____ 5. They lived happily ever *after*.

_____ 6. I have not seen them *since*, but we have talked on the phone a few times.

_____ 7. They did not know *about* that book.

_____ 8. There is a light *outside* the door of the confessional.

_____ 9. God's grace will see us *through*; His mercy never fails.

_____ 10. *Through* the window, we saw that our company had arrived.

Lesson 74: PREPOSITIONS, CONJUNCTIONS, INTERJECTIONS

Correct Use of Prepositions: *Between / Among* and *Beside / Besides*

> The preposition **between** is used when speaking of **two** persons, things, or groups.
> The preposition **among** is used when speaking of **three or more** persons, things, or groups.

> The preposition **beside** means **at the side of or next to**.
> The preposition **besides** means **in addition to**.

She could not decide **between** the blue hat and the red one.
There were two black lambs **among** the sheep.

The new girl sat **beside** me.
There are four new students **besides** her.

Exercise 74A: Circle the correct preposition in the parentheses.

1. There are more reasons (beside, besides) that.
2. The three Scribes plotted (between, among) themselves.
3. An angel appeared (beside, besides) the empty tomb.
4. My brother and I share a room (between, among) us.
5. Place the book (beside, besides) the computer.
6. There are three Gospels (beside, besides) St. Matthew's.
7. A rich man divided his land (between, among) his three servants.
8. There is a strong bond (between, among) a mother and her child.
9. There are many good works you can do (beside, besides) giving money to the poor.
10. The jury discussed the case (between, among) themselves.

Exercise 74B: Diagram the following sentence.

Besides the two new students, three graduates circulated among the crowd.

PREPOSITIONS, CONJUNCTIONS, INTERJECTIONS

Lesson 75

Correct Use of Prepositions: *In / Into* and *From / Off*

> The preposition *in* indicates a position within.
> The preposition *into* indicates motion or a change of position.

> The preposition *from* indicates receiving from.
> The preposition *off* means "away from."

The Eucharist is **in** the tabernacle.
Father places the ciborium **into** the tabernacle.

We received the rosaries **from** the nun.
The children stepped **off** the porch.

Exercise 75A: Circle the correct preposition in the parentheses.

1. He borrowed the book (from, off) the library.
2. Christ will gather His flock (in, into) His Kingdom.
3. The new neighbors moved (in, into) the house last week.
4. He poured the water (in, into) the basin.
5. Take that book (from, off) the shelf.
6. Mom removed a small splinter (from, off) my finger.
7. Please load the dishes (in, into) the dishwasher.
8. He took the wrench (from, off) Mark.
9. The ball rolled (from, off) the table.
10. I cracked two eggs (in, into) a frying pan.

Exercise 75B: Diagram the following sentence.

Dave took the picture of the mountains off the wall.

Lesson 76: PREPOSITIONS, CONJUNCTIONS, INTERJECTIONS

Correct Use of Prepositions: *Differ With / Differ From* and *Angry With / Angry At*

> ***Differ with*** indicates disagreement or a difference of opinion.
> ***Differ from*** indicates differences in characteristics between persons or things.

> One is ***angry with*** a person but ***angry at*** a thing.

I **differ with** you about the value of this painting.
The children **differ from** each other in personality.

She is **angry with** Bob.
They were **angry at** the election results.

Exercise 76: Circle the correct words in parentheses.

1. You differ (with, from) me on many issues.

2. Grandpa was never angry (with, at) anyone.

3. In what ways does the new Mass differ (with, from) the old?

4. My mother is angry (with, at) me for not doing my chores.

5. Joe differs (with, from) Tom about the best football team.

6. Just because it is raining, you should not be angry (with, at) the weather.

7. Those two friends differ (with, from) each other in many aspects of their appearance.

8. How did the teachings of Jesus differ (with, from) those of the Scribes and Pharisees?

9. Jesus was angry (with, at) the way the money changers were desecrating the temple.

10. Father Daly's homilies differ (with, from) Father Avery's, but both are wonderful.

11. How does this picture differ (with, from) that one?

12. Are you angry (with, at) your brother?

PREPOSITIONS, CONJUNCTIONS, INTERJECTIONS

Lesson 77

Adjectival and Adverbial Prepositional Phrases

> A **prepositional phrase** that relates to a noun or a pronoun is called an **adjectival phrase**. An **adjectival phrase** functions as an adjective and answers the questions *which one? what kind? how many?* or *whose?*

> A **prepositional phrase** that relates to a verb is an **adverbial phrase**. An **adverbial phrase** functions as an adverb and usually answers the questions *when? where? how?* or *why?*

> A sentence may contain several prepositional phrases. The prepositional phrases may relate to the same word, or each phrase may relate to a different word.

At every Mass, we celebrate the mystery **of** the Holy Eucharist.

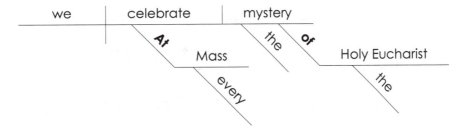

Exercise 77: Circle the prepositional phrases in each sentence. Above each phrase, write ADJ for an adjectival phrase, and ADV for an adverbial phrase.

1. A cry came from the woods.
2. Jesus led them to a high mountain, and He was transfigured before them.
3. Christ was nailed to a cross for our sins.
4. Pray for us at the hour of our death.
5. Father Hanlon stood behind the altar.
6. Saint Thomas More wore a hair shirt under his clothes.
7. At the age of fifteen, Saint Therese entered the convent.

Lesson 78: PREPOSITIONS, CONJUNCTIONS, INTERJECTIONS

Conjunctions—Definition and Functions

> A **conjunction** is the part of speech that connects words, phrases, or clauses in a sentence.

> A **conjunction** may connect **words** that are nouns and pronouns **that perform the same function** in a sentence, and they may connect adjectives, verbs, and adverbs.

> A **conjunction** may connect **phrases**. A phrase is a group of words that, combined, perform a function in a sentence. A **prepositional phrase**, for example, modifies a noun, a pronoun, or a verb.
> A **phrase** does not contain a predicate and a subject.

> A **conjunction** may connect **independent clauses**. A clause is a part of a sentence that contains a predicate and a subject.

conjunction connects words that perform the same function
subject | **subject (nouns that perform the same function)**
Peter and Paul were two of the early founders of the Church.

conjunction connects adjectival phrases
adjectival phrase | **adjectival phrase**
People of all nations and of all races received the disciples.

conjunction connects adverbial phrases
adverbial phrase | **adverbial phrase**
They taught people about Our Lord and about His message of salvation.

conjunction connects independant clauses
clause | **clause**
They sometimes met with controversy, but they never wavered from the truth.

PREPOSITIONS, CONJUNCTIONS, INTERJECTIONS
Lesson 79

Coordinate and Correlative Conjunctions Connect Words and Phrases

> A **coordinate conjunction** is the part of speech that connects words, phrases, and clauses. **Correlative conjunctions** are coordinate conjunctions that are used in pairs.

Coordinate Conjunctions
and   nor   yet
or   but

Correlative Conjunctions
either…or   both…and
neither…nor   not only…but also

Coordinate conjunctions connect words that perform the same function.

subjects   **predicates**   **direct objects**

Peter and Paul preached and spread Christ's words and their meaning.

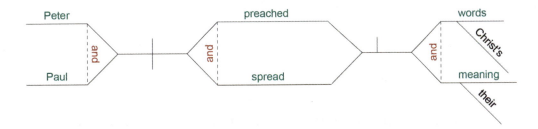

Coordinate conjunctions connect adjectival phrases.

The hardships of their travels or of people's resistance could not diminish their efforts.

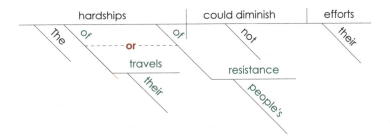

Coordinate conjunctions connect adverbial phrases.

They preached not only with belief in their mission but also with absolute reliance upon God.

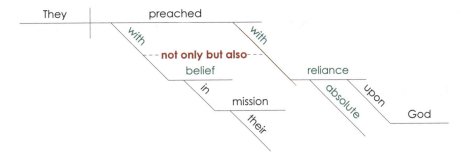

Saint Thomas More, Pray for us!   J.M.J.   *English 8 for Young Catholics*

Lesson 79: PREPOSITIONS, CONJUNCTIONS, INTERJECTIONS

Exercise 79A: Circle the conjunctions and underline the words that the conjunctions connect. On the lines to the right, write the function of the words you underlined: subjects, predicates, indirect objects, direct objects, or subjective complements.

1. The religious bookstore sells (both) rosaries (and) religious medals. _____direct objects_____
2. St. Joan of Arc was brave and determined in battle. _____
3. St. Joan inspired and encouraged the soldiers. _____
4. Missionaries have suffered hardship and famine to preach the Gospel. _____
5. Not only Anne, but also Angela plans to enter the convent. _____
6. Our Blessed Lady neither sinned, nor desired to sin. _____
7. Mark will become either a priest or a religious brother. _____
8. Both prayers and works are necessary to gain salvation. _____
9. Sally lost the argument but gained experience in debating. _____
10. Mr. Richards gave Tom and Michael a tennis lesson. _____

Exercise 79B: Circle the conjunctions and underline the phrases that the conjunctions connect. On the lines to the right, write ADJ for an adjectival phrase or ADV for an adverbial phrase.

1. Place the statue <u>on the shelf</u> (and) <u>beside the Bible</u>. _____ADV_____
2. We play baseball in the summer, but not on rainy days. _____
3. His was a jacket with lapels but without buttons. _____
4. We will go either to Baltimore or to Washington for Easter. _____
5. A walk around the lake or on the mountain trail sounds great. _____
6. The panel counted the votes both for the proposition and against it. _____
7. Dan swam to the pier and around it. _____
8. The vigil for priests and for missionaries was well-attended. _____
9. Coffee with milk but without sugar is her preference. _____
10. I read either from the Bible or from a spiritual book every day. _____

PREPOSITIONS, CONJUNCTIONS, INTERJECTIONS
Lesson 80

Coordinate Conjunctions Connect Independent Clauses

Coordinate conjunctions may connect words, phrases, and **independent clauses**.
A **clause** is a part of a sentence that contains a predicate and a subject.
An **independent clause** is part of a sentence that can stand alone as a complete thought.

Sentences with independent clauses:

We must feed this crowd, **or** they will starve.
We have gathered only five loaves of bread, **and** one boy gave us two fishes.
There was a multitude on the hillside, **but** everyone received enough food.

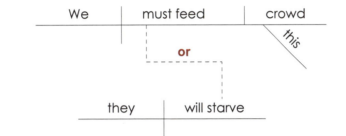

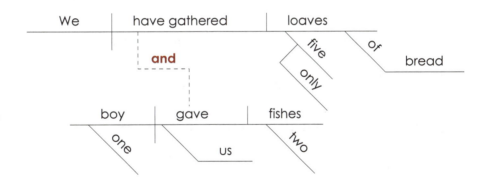

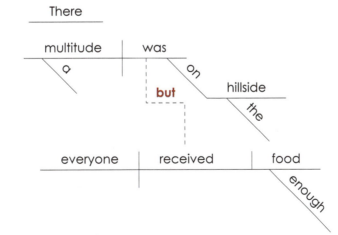

Lesson 80: PREPOSITIONS, CONJUNCTIONS, INTERJECTIONS

Exercise 80A: Circle the conjunction(s) in each sentence. Write P above the predicate and S above the subject in each independent clause.

Example: The trumpets blared, **(and)** everyone stood at once.
(S: trumpets, P: blared; S: everyone, P: stood)

1. You must take these commandments to My people, **and** they must abide by them.

2. **Either** Mary will go with us, **or** she will stay home with her cousins.

3. The children told of the vision, **but** the people did not believe them.

4. I would play cards with you, **but** I must study for a test.

5. Her shoes are too small for her, **and** they do not fit her sister either.

6. They **neither** listened to Moses **nor** obeyed God's Laws.

7. I should leave now, **or** I will be late for Mass.

8. At first, she wanted pink wallpaper for her room, **but** she decided on yellow paint instead.

9. Helen will do her math homework first, **and** she will study history later.

10. Danny will play the violin, **and** Myra will accompany him on the piano.

Exercise 80B: Diagram sentences 9 and 10 from the above exercise.

PREPOSITIONS, CONJUNCTIONS, INTERJECTIONS

Lesson 81

Subordinate Conjunctions Connect Dependent Clauses to Independent Clauses

> A **clause** is a part of a sentence that contains a predicate and a subject.
> An **independent clause** is part of a sentence that **can** stand alone as a complete thought.
> A **dependent clause** is part of a sentence that **cannot** stand alone as a complete thought.
> A **subordinate conjunction** introduces a **dependent clause** and connects it to an **independent clause**.

Some Common Subordinate Conjunctions

although	if	so	that	though
because	provided	than	then	unless
for				

Word Groups Used as Subordinate Conjunctions

as well as	in order that	provided that
as if	inasmuch as	so that

⎧ independent clause ⎫ ⎧ dependent clause ⎫   ⎧ dependent clause ⎫ ⎧ independent clause ⎫
I will love all men **because** Christ did.   **Unless** we pray often, we cannot expect eternal life.

Independent Clause

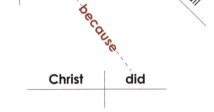

Dependent Clause

Independent Clause

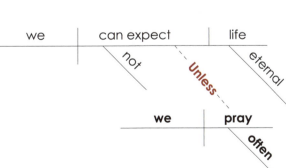

Dependent Clause

Note: When you diagram a subordinate conjunction, write the conjunction on the line, not through the line.

Lesson 81: PREPOSITIONS, CONJUNCTIONS, INTERJECTIONS

Exercise 81A: Circle each dependent clause, and underline the independent clause in each sentence.

Example: <u>You must pray daily</u> (if you wish to overcome temptation.)

1. I love to attend Mass because I can receive Jesus in Holy Communion.
2. We will clean the house so Mom can rest.
3. We will do our chores now, so that we may play basketball later.
4. We shall have a Rosary procession provided that it does not rain.
5. Although she is busy, she finds time to help the sick.
6. If they became engaged, we would plan for the wedding.
7. We homeschool so that we may become well educated in the Catholic Faith.
8. Although Jesus worked many miracles, some leaders rejected Him.
9. Mom will take us to the zoo today provided that we clean our room.
10. Because so many people came to the novena, Father heard Confessions.
11. Unless there is a Holy Hour on Friday night, we shall go to the movies.
12. The children helped their grandmother clean the house as if it were their own home.

Exercise 81B: Diagram the following sentence.

Although we have a busy schedule, we pray the Rosary in the evening.

PREPOSITIONS, CONJUNCTIONS, INTERJECTIONS

Lesson 82

Conjunctive Adverbs

A **conjunctive adverb** is a word that functions as an adverb and a conjunction.
A **conjunctive adverb** functions as a **coordinate conjunction** when it connects independent clauses.
A **conjunctive adverb** functions as a **subordinate conjunction** when it connects a dependent clause to an independent clause. (A dependent clause is part of a sentence that cannot stand alone as a complete thought.)

Conjunctive Adverbs as Coordinate Conjunctions

also	however	notwithstanding	therefore
consequently	moreover	still	thus
furthermore	nevertheless	subsequently	

He did not know the meaning of the word; **therefore**, he referred to the dictionary.

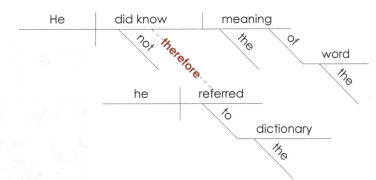

Conjunctive Adverbs as Subordinate Conjunctions

after	before	until	where
as	since	when	while

We shall say a prayer **before** we start our lessons.

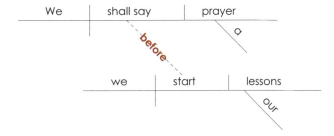

Lesson 82: PREPOSITIONS, CONJUNCTIONS, INTERJECTIONS

Exercise 82A: Circle the conjunction in each sentence. On the lines to the right, write whether it is a coordinate or a subordinate conjunction.

1. I am tired; nevertheless, I will stay awake to pray for one more hour. _____
2. Jesus prayed until the soldiers came for Him. _____
3. Peter denied Him three times before the rooster crowed. _____
4. The martyrs were afraid; however, they did not renounce the Faith. _____
5. While he was asleep, an angel appeared to him in a dream. _____
6. She entered the convent; consequently, she became a nun. _____
7. When the storm arose, they woke Him up. _____
8. She had no idea where she might have forgotten her purse. _____
9. I received a scholarship from Christendom College; therefore, I will go there this year. _____
10. St. Jane de Chantal was a wife and mother; however, later in her life, she founded a religious order. _____

Exercise 82B: Diagram the following sentence.

They knew the right road after they consulted their map.

PREPOSITIONS, CONJUNCTIONS, INTERJECTIONS
Lesson 83

Correct Use of *Like* / *As* and *Like* / *As If*

> The word *like* is a **preposition**; it is followed by a word or a phrase.
> The words *as* and *as if* are **conjunctions**; they are followed by clauses.

Mary looks **like** her mother.

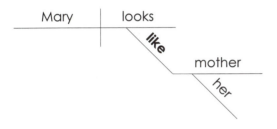

Mary speaks **as** her mother speaks.

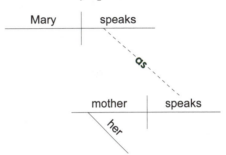

Act **like** a man, my son.
Her handkerchief smells **like** lavender.
Like a fish, Helen swims across the pool.

Sue acts **as if** she knows the answer.
Love one another **as** I have loved you.
This vine spreads **as** weeds do.

Exercise 83: Circle the correct word(s) in parentheses.

1. He spoke Spanish (like, as if) he were a native.
2. Clean your room (like, as) your mother directs.
3. (Like, as) her mother, Loretta is very beautiful and very kind.
4. The apostles did (like, as) Christ commanded them.
5. The church looked (like, as if) it had been renovated.
6. Michael acts very much (like, as) his pious older brother.
7. During St. Teresa of Avila's ecstasies, it seemed to her (like, as if) no time had passed.
8. Do unto others (like, as) I have done unto you.
9. He is tall (like, as) his father.
10. This plant grows (like, as) a vine.
11. (Like, As) a deer looks for water, my soul searches for You, my Lord.
12. Tim became a coach (like, as) his father and his grandfather before him.

Lesson 84: PREPOSITIONS, CONJUNCTIONS, INTERJECTIONS

Interjections

An **interjection** is the part of speech that shows a strong or sudden emotion. **Interjections** may express such emotions as surprise, pain, wonder, longing, sadness, sorrow, joy, impatience, or wonder.

An **interjection** is not grammatically connected to other words in a sentence.

An author may choose to use either an exclamation point or a period at the end of a sentence that is preceded or followed by an interjection.

Some Common Interjections

Ah!	*Good-bye!*	*Hooray!*	*Sh!*
Alas!	*Hark!*	*Lo!*	*Ugh!*
Alleluia!	*Hello!*	*Oh!*	*Well!*
Bravo!	*Hey!*	*Ouch!*	*Wow!*

Hooray! The parade is here.
Ouch! I stubbed my toe.
Ah, how cute your new baby is!

Exercise 84: Circle the interjection(s) in each sentence.

1. Look! The pope is coming down the street. Hooray!
2. Oh, how beautiful the sunset is!
3. Hush! The concert is about to begin.
4. Excellent! You received an "A" on your report.
5. That performance was wonderful! Bravo!
6. Alleluia, the Lord has risen. Alleluia! Alleluia!
7. Oh, you simply must read this new book!
8. Wow! That is quite an accomplishment!
9. Say! Is that a real diamond?
10. Well, that was quite a surprise!

CHAPTER 7

CLAUSES AND SENTENCES

CLAUSES AND SENTENCES

CLAUSES AND SENTENCES

Chapter Outline

CHAPTER SEVEN

I. **Clauses defined**
   A. Independent clauses
   B. Dependent clauses
      1. Adjective clauses
      2. Adverb clauses
      3. Noun clauses

II. **Sentences**
   A. Essential elements
   B. Natural and inverted order
   C. Types according to use
      1. Declarative
      2. Interrogative
      3. Imperative
      4. Exclamatory
   D. Types according to form
      1. Simple
      2. Compound
      3. Complex

III. **Run-on sentences and sentence fragments**

Lesson 85 — CLAUSES AND SENTENCES

Clauses

A **clause** is a part of a sentence that contains a subject and a predicate.

An **independent clause** expresses a complete thought that can stand alone.
Independent clauses are connected by coordinate conjunctions.
A **coordinate conjunction** is the part of speech that connects words, phrases, and independent clauses.

We have gathered five loaves of bread, **and** *one boy gave us two fishes,* **but** *that is not enough for this crowd.*

- *We have gathered five loaves of bread* — independent clause
- **and** — coordinate conjunction
- *one boy gave us two fishes* — independent clause
- **but** — coordinate conjunction
- *that is not enough for this crowd* — independent clause

A **dependent clause** does not express a complete thought, and it cannot stand alone.
A **dependent clause** is introduced by and connected to an independent clause by a subordinate conjunction (including conjunctive adverbs), a relative pronoun, a relative adjective, or a relative adverb.

The disciples were distraught **because** *there was not enough food for the crowd of five thousand.*

- *The disciples were distraught* — independent clause
- **because** — subordinate conjunction
- *there was not enough food for the crowd of five thousand* — dependent clause

Type of Dependent Clause	Function	Introduced by	
Adjective Clause	Modifies a noun or a pronoun	Relative Pronoun	*who, whose, whom, which, that*
		Two Subordinate Conjunctions	*when* and *where*
Adverb Clause	Modifies a verb, an adjective, or another adverb	Subordinate Conjunction	*although, because, for, if, provided, so, than, that, then, though, unless,*
		Conjunctive Adverb	*after, as, before, since, until, when, where, while*
Noun Clause	Any noun function	Various Words	*that, if, how, however, what, whatever, when, where, whether, whether or not, which, whichever, who, whom, whoever, whomever, whose, why*

CLAUSES AND SENTENCES

Lesson 85

Exercise 85: Underline the dependent clause in each sentence. Write P above the predicate and S above the subject in both the dependent clause and the independent clause.

Example: My brother, <u>who is the editor of our newsletter</u>, hopes the publication will make a difference.
(S above "brother", S above "who", P above "is", P above "hopes")

Example: John told us <u>where the church was</u>.
(S above "John", P above "told", S above "church", P above "was")

1. If you take the time to pray about it, you surely will make the right decision.

2. After the angel appeared to him in a dream, Joseph left for Egypt.

3. Whatever you do, it must be morally good.

4. It is a fact that the Trinity is a mystery.

5. Some nuns work out in the world, while others are cloistered.

6. This prayer, which Mother Teresa recited every day, soothes my soul.

7. Whether or not he planned it that way, he arrived just in time.

8. Father Martin explained how we may obtain sanctifying grace.

9. God kept His promise that He would send His only Son.

10. Unless we notify you otherwise, Mass will be held in the side chapel next week.

11. Washington, DC, which is the capital of the United States, welcomes tourists from all over the world.

12. He did not say why he decided to go to Chicago for the weekend.

Saint Thomas More, Pray for us!

Lesson 86: CLAUSES AND SENTENCES

Adjective Clauses

> An **adjective clause** is a dependent clause that functions as an adjective to describe or limit a noun or a pronoun.
>
> An **adjective clause** is introduced by a relative pronoun (*who, whom, whose, which, that*) or by the subordinate conjunctions *when* or *where*.

Saint Isaac Jogues, **who** <u>was a Jesuit</u>, labored among the Mohawks.
The ones **which** <u>were on the top shelf</u> were most expensive.
The parish organized a retirement banquet for Msgr. Reynolds, **whom** <u>they greatly admire</u>.
We went to Mass at St. Peter's, **where** <u>many popes are buried</u>.
It was a turbulent time **when** <u>many died for their faith</u>.

(The slanted line indicates that the modifier of the noun functions as an adjective.)

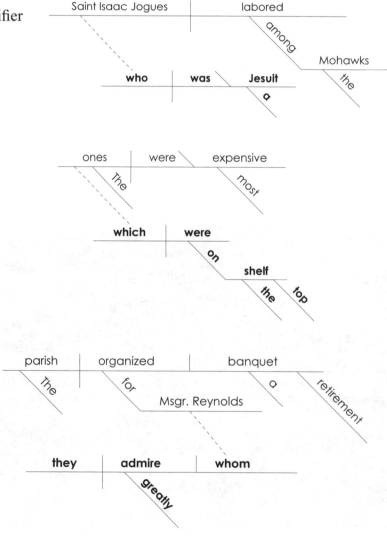

156   English 8 for Young Catholics

CLAUSES AND SENTENCES

Lesson 86

Exercise 86A: Underline the adjective clause in each sentence. Circle the noun that the clause modifies.

1. St. John Lateran, <u>which is one of the many churches in Rome</u>, is the pope's own cathedral.

2. That church has a chapel <u>where the Eucharist is perpetually exposed</u>.

3. Children <u>who are disciplined</u> are guided toward a life of virtue.

4. St. Thomas Aquinas is the saint <u>who explained the doctrine of Transubstantiation</u>.

5. The Pantheon, <u>which was a pagan temple</u>, is now a place of Christian worship.

6. St. Peter, <u>who was martyred in 64 A. D.</u>, was the first pope.

7. The church was filled with people <u>who anxiously awaited the arrival of the pope</u>.

8. People <u>who travel to Lourdes</u> see the miraculous waters.

9. The Catholic Church is the only church <u>that can trace its beginning to Jesus Christ</u>.

10. A plenary indulgence is one <u>that completely removes the punishment of sin</u>.

11. Paris, <u>which is the most famous city in France</u>, contains many museums.

12. St. Jane de Chantal, <u>who founded the Visitation Sisters</u>, was also a widow and mother.

13. The Creed is the part of the Mass <u>that proclaims the Church's central beliefs</u>.

14. A lectionary is a book <u>that contains all the readings for the Mass</u>.

15. The storm <u>that frightened the disciples</u> was calmed by a command from Jesus.

Exercise 86B: Diagram the following sentence.

Our bishop, who will celebrate Mass at 11:00, will be the honored guest at the banquet.

Lesson 87: CLAUSES AND SENTENCES

Adverb Clauses

> An **adverb clause** is a dependent clause that functions as an adverb to modify a verb, an adjective, or another adverb.
> An **adverb clause** is introduced by a subordinate conjunction or a conjunctive adverb.
> An **adverb clause** often tells *time*, *place*, *manner*, *cause*, or *purpose*.

Time — after, as, before, since, then, until, when, while
  After we left the church, we had breakfast.
  Henry has wanted to become a priest **since** he was very young.

Place — where
  We will go **where** You lead us.

Manner — as, as if, as though, than
  Claudia plans to study French **as** her sister did.
  The student answered the question **as though** he were an expert on the subject.

Cause — as, because, for, since, so, though
  We will move this plant to an interior room **because** it needs indirect sunlight.
  Since he studied hard for his test, he received an excellent grade.

Purpose — so, so that, that
  We will go outdoors **so that** we can get some exercise.
  Christ came **that** we might have abundant life.

(The slanted line indicates that the modifier of the verb functions as an adverb.)

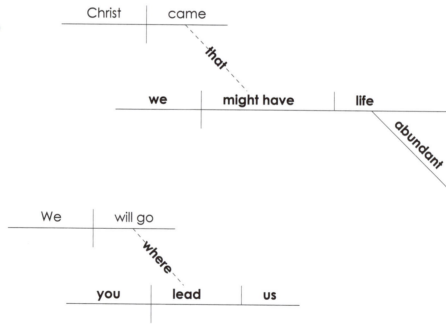

CLAUSES AND SENTENCES

Lesson 87

Exercise 87A: Underline the adverb clause in each sentence. Circle the word that it modifies.

1. Mary answered "Yes," because she loved God.
2. Since the pope seemed trapped at Avignon, this period is known as the Avignon captivity.
3. John left the church when the Mass was over.
4. When you visit Rome, you should make a visit to the Sistine Chapel.
5. The well-trained police dog stopped where the money was buried.
6. As if her life depended on it, the saint firmly held the crucifix.
7. Jonah thought himself a coward after the fish had swallowed him.
8. The confessional in the church is occupied if the red light is on.
9. When the green light is on above the confessional, the penitent may enter.
10. Mom will drive him to the library because he missed the bus.
11. When I smelled incense, I knew that Mass was about to begin.
12. I will visit my grandmother after I finish saying the Rosary.
13. John reached the tomb first because he could run faster than Peter.
14. They stayed until the parade ended.
15. Because you have paid attention, you will complete that assignment successfully.

Exercise 87B: Diagram the following sentence.

You may have dessert when you finish your dinner.

Saint Thomas More, Pray for us! J.M.J. English 8 for Young Catholics

Lesson 88: CLAUSES AND SENTENCES

Noun Clauses

> A **noun clause** is a dependent clause that may perform any function of a noun.
> A **noun clause** is introduced by various words.

Words Used to Introduce Noun Clauses: *that, if, how, however, what, whatever, when, where, whether, whether or not, which, whichever, who, whom, whoever, whomever, whose, why*

Functions of Noun Clauses

subject   **That** he respected his parents was evident to everyone.

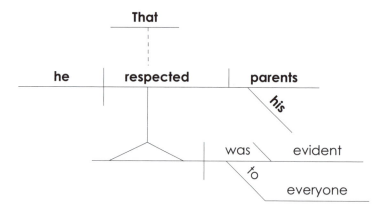

subjective complement   The question is **whether or not** she will participate in the race.

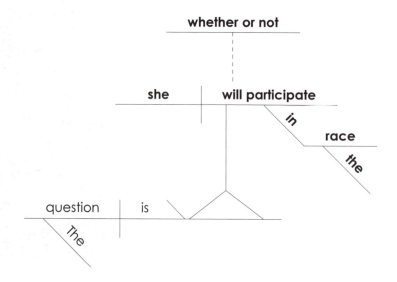

CLAUSES AND SENTENCES

Lesson 88

Functions of Noun Clauses (continued)

appositive Do not confuse appositive noun clauses with adjective clauses. An appositive noun clause *takes the place of a noun*; an adjective clause *modifies a noun or a pronoun*.

The fact **that** the priesthood is a special vocation remains true.

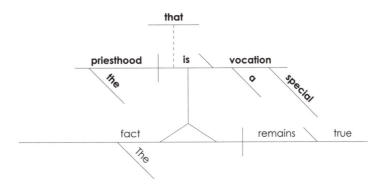

direct object You may choose **whichever** appeals to you.

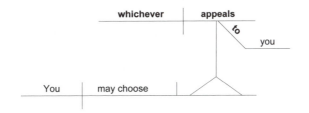

indirect object The coach will give **whoever** finishes today's drills a special ribbon.

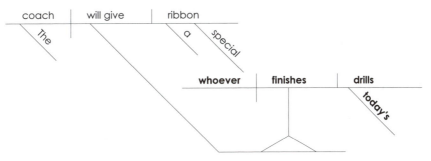

object of a preposition He is clear about **what** he values.

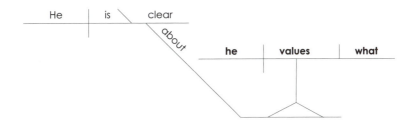

Lesson 88: CLAUSES AND SENTENCES

Exercise 88A: Underline the noun clause in each sentence. On the lines to the right, write S if the clause functions as a subject, SC if a subjective complement, or A if an appositive.

1. What God tells us in the Bible helps us to lead a moral life. _____
2. Whatever caused the outburst was not known. _____
3. The greatest proof of Christ's divinity is that He arose from the dead. _____
4. The children immediately obeyed the command that they pick up their toys. _____
5. The priest's chief concern is that souls will be saved. _____
6. The fact that so many people have been cured at Lourdes is amazing. _____
7. That St. Peter was the first pope is not denied. _____
8. One requirement is that the president should be a good moral leader. _____
9. What keeps us in God's grace is frequent reception of the sacraments. _____
10. Are you proud of the fact that your brother has been ordained a priest? _____
11. Our Creed affirms our belief that God became man. _____
12. The question is why the rich young man walked away. _____
13. Whoever keeps My commandments will have eternal life. _____
14. The Church's teaching is that Christ will come again. _____
15. The report that the pope has written a new encyclical is true. _____

Exercise 88B: Diagram the following sentence.

That Robert served at the Easter Mass greatly pleased his family.

CLAUSES AND SENTENCES

Lesson 88

Exercise 88C: Underline the noun clause in each sentence. On the lines to the right, write DO if the clause functions as a direct object, IO if an Indirect Object, or OP if an object of a preposition.

1. Do you know that there have been thousands of miracles? _____
2. The Sacred Heart League will send whoever wants one a liturgical calendar. _____
3. Have you ever read about what Father Damien did for the lepers? _____
4. We believe that Christ died for the salvation of our souls. _____
5. God promised that He would send a Redeemer. _____
6. The children were amazed at what the priest told them. _____
7. Our Lord gives graces to whoever asks for them. _____
8. The shopkeeper gives whatever needs it a good dusting and polishing. _____
9. The brothers were greatly affected by what they saw at Lourdes. _____
10. Our Lady said that we should pray the Rosary. _____
11. Your view of the pope depends upon where you sit. _____
12. They will buy whoever needs them a new pair of shoes. _____
13. The father had no thought except that he must save his child. _____
14. Remember that virtue is a habit of the soul. _____
15. The priest said that everyone must receive the sacraments. _____

Exercise 88D: Diagram the following sentence.

The Church teaches that Christ died for all men.

Lesson 89: CLAUSES AND SENTENCES

Sentences—Essential Elements

> A **sentence** is a group of words that expresses a complete thought.
> Every sentence must have a **subject and a predicate**.
> Sometimes the **subject** is not expressed, but the **predicate** is always expressed.

Sentence with an expressed subject   **We** respectfully stand for the bishop.

Sentence with an understood subject   Stand for the bishop.

> The **subject** is the part of the sentence which names the person, place, thing, or idea about which the sentence makes a statement.
> A **compound subject** is two or more nouns or pronouns that act as one subject.
> The **complete subject** is the subject and all its modifiers.

Compound subject   The entire **congregation** and the **priests** respectfully stand for the bishop.

Complete subject   **The entire congregation and the priests** respectfully stand for the bishop.

> The **predicate** is the part of the sentence which tells something about the subject by expressing action, being, or state of being.
> A **compound predicate** is two or more predicates that tell something about the subject.
> The **complete predicate** is the predicate and all its modifiers and complements.

Compound predicate   The entire congregation respectfully **stands** and **applauds** the bishop.

Complete predicate   The entire congregation **respectfully stands and applauds the bishop**.

The entire congregation and the priests respectfully stand and applaud the bishop and the cardinal with fervor.

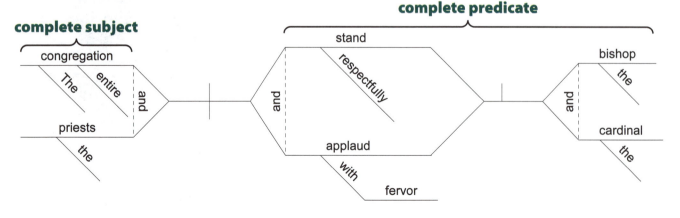

CLAUSES AND SENTENCES

Lesson 89

Exercise 89A: Circle the complete subject and underline the complete predicate in each sentence.

1. St. Matthew and St. Mark wrote Gospels.
2. The apostles evangelized and baptized many people.
3. Sloth, envy, and greed are just three of the seven cardinal sins.
4. A group of girls entered the convent.
5. The search for the true Cross spread and lasted hundreds of years.
6. A vine-covered abbey stood on top of the hill.
7. During Advent, three purple candles and one pink one are placed in a wreath.
8. The baby gurgled and cooed at his father.
9. After Mass, we should thank and adore Our Lord.
10. Today is the first day of summer.
11. Mary and her little sister, Agnes, knelt and prayed for the soul of their grandmother.
12. Sacraments are the means to sanctifying grace.
13. The third Gospel in the Bible and the Acts of the Apostles were written by St. Luke.
14. Priests and bishops instruct and lead the faithful.
15. The priest acts as a mediator between God and man.

Exercise 89B: Diagram the following sentence.

The raging wind and relentless rain battered and thoroughly drenched the crew of the fishing boat.

Lesson 90

CLAUSES AND SENTENCES

Sentences—Natural and Inverted Order

> A sentence is in the **natural order** when the subject comes before the predicate. Even if modifiers such as adjectives, adverbs, or prepositional phrases come before the subject, the sentence is still in the natural order.

Sentences in which the **subject** comes before the predicate are in the **natural order**.

      Christ rose on Easter Sunday.
      On Easter Sunday, **Christ** rose.

      The good **thief** and the unrepentant **one** hung on either side of Jesus.
      On either side of Jesus, the good **thief** and the unrepentant **one** hung.

> A sentence is in the **inverted order** when the predicate or part of the predicate (the helping verb) comes before the subject.
> Questions that begin with a predicate or a helping verb are always in the inverted order.
> Sentences that begin with the introductory words "There" or "Here" are always in the inverted order.

Sentences in which the predicate comes before the **subject** are in the **inverted order**.

      Over the field hovered the **helicopter**.
      Did **you** see the helicopter over the field?
      There is a **helicopter** above the field.

Exercise 90: Circle the complete subject(s) and underline the complete predicate(s) in each sentence. On the lines to the right, write whether the sentence is in the natural or inverted order.

1. You can receive many graces by going to Mass.   _____
2. Did you hear the great news?   _____
3. Some people prefer a quiet life.   _____
4. Arched over the hills is a beautiful rainbow.   _____
5. Below a cliff runs a swirling river.   _____
6. High above us, puffy white clouds passed by.   _____
7. Here is a book from the library.   _____
8. Who will attend the conference?   _____
9. By their works you will know them.   _____
10. On the trapeze sat the circus clown.   _____

CLAUSES AND SENTENCES

Lesson 91

Types of Sentences According to Use

The **function** (use or purpose) of a sentence determines the type of sentence that it is. Depending on its function, a sentence may be **declarative**, **interrogative**, **imperative**, or **exclamatory**.

A **declarative sentence** makes a statement and ends with a period.
An **interrogative sentence** asks a question and ends with a question mark.
An **imperative sentence** makes a request or gives a command and ends with a period.
An **exclamatory sentence** expresses a strong emotion and ends with an exclamation point.

Declarative	The first pope was Saint Peter.
Interrogative	Who was the first pope?
Imperative	Read the lives of the saints.
Exclamatory	How inspiring they are!

Exercise 91: On the lines to the left, write the sentence type. On the lines to the right, insert the correct end punctuation.

1. _____ St. Peter's is the largest church in the world _____
2. _____ Who wrote *Introduction to the Devout Life* _____
3. _____ The Crusades were not very successful _____
4. _____ I will shout to the world that I would rather die than deny Our Lord _____
5. _____ Was St. Elizabeth of Hungary a queen _____
6. _____ "Take up your cross and follow Me _____ "
7. _____ Please remain quiet during the Mass _____
8. _____ Do not run on the wet pavement _____
9. _____ Look out _____
10. _____ Michelangelo was an extraordinarily talented man _____
11. _____ The fire is spreading; we must all leave now _____
12. _____ Just beyond the field stands the convent _____

Saint Thomas More, Pray for us!

Lesson 92: CLAUSES AND SENTENCES

Types of Sentences According to Form

> A **simple sentence** expresses one complete thought.
> A **simple** sentence contains a subject and its modifiers and a predicate and its modifiers.
> The **subject** and the **predicate** in a simple sentence may be simple or compound.

subject   **predicate**

St. Therese, a saintly French girl, <u>entered</u> the convent at fifteen.
St. Therese of Lisieux and **St. Teresa of Avila** <u>were</u> Carmelite nuns.

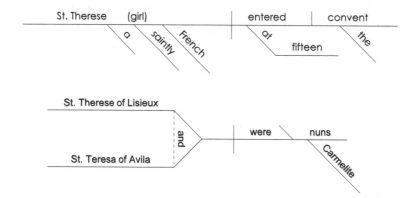

> A **compound sentence** contains two or more complete thoughts. Each complete thought is an **independent clause**.
> In a **compound sentence**, independent clauses may be joined by a coordinating conjunction (*and, or, but*).
> A comma precedes the conjunction in a compound sentence.
> A semicolon may replace the conjunction. In a diagram, the semicolon is placed on the same line as the conjunction it replaces.

independent clause   **conjunction**   **independent clause**

Saint Dominic had great devotion to our Blessed Mother, and he taught the use of the Rosary in her honor.

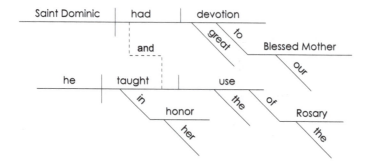

CLAUSES AND SENTENCES

Lesson 92

Types of Sentences According to Form (continued)

> A **complex sentence** contains one complete thought (**independent clause**) and at least one incomplete thought (**dependent clause**), which cannot stand alone.
> A comma follows a dependent clause that begins a sentence.

dependent clause

St. Dominic, who was the founder of the Dominicans, taught the use of the Rosary.

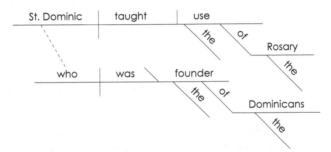

Exercise 92: On the lines to the right, write whether the sentence is Simple, Compound, or Complex.

1. Each of the seven sacraments must contain proper form and matter. _____
2. The soul gets its nourishment from the grace of the sacraments and prayer. _____
3. The home of the pope is at the Vatican, but in the summer, he resides at Castel Gandolfo. _____
4. Monte Cassino was a famous Benedictine monastery which was destroyed during World War II. _____
5. Have you visited the town of Fatima where Our Blessed Lady appeared? _____
6. I am the vine, and you are the branches. _____
7. Faith and hope are two of the most important virtues. _____
8. In 451 A.D., the Council of Chalcedon convened. _____
9. Mary received the award, and her family was proud of her. _____
10. A child cannot go to Confession until he has reached the age of reason. _____
11. When a penitent receives absolution, his sins are forgiven. _____
12. The following day, they had a beautiful but simple wedding. _____

Lesson 93: CLAUSES AND SENTENCES

Run-On Sentences and Sentence Fragments

> A **run-on sentence** contains two or more independent clauses that are not connected by a conjunction or a semicolon.
> A run-on "sentence" is not a sentence; it is incorrect writing.

> A **sentence fragment** is an incomplete sentence.
> A **sentence fragment** may be a group of words that is missing a predicate or a subject.
> A **sentence fragment** may be a dependent clause, which cannot stand alone to express a complete thought.

Exercise 93: On the lines, write whether the numbered sentence is Complete, a Run-on, or a Fragment.

1 Robert began reading library books. **2** When he was very young. **3** By the fourth grade, he was reading one book every week. **4** Robert preferred historical novels. **5** Even now, he reads historical novels, it helps not only with history, but with vocabulary as well. **6** His knowledge of history helps him to put the stories of saints in perspective. **7** By understanding the customs and lifestyles that were prevalent at the time the saint lived.
8 Authors use different styles, they include words they find are important to the story. **9** Helps Robert learn new words all the time. **10** He looks up words that are new to him. **11** His compositions improve. **12** Because he uses a variety of effective words to express himself clearly.

1. _____
2. _____
3. _____
4. _____
5. _____
6. _____
7. _____
8. _____
9. _____
10. _____
11. _____
12. _____

HANDBOOK

Capitalization

1. Capitalize the **first word** in a sentence, including direct quotations.

    St. Paul told the Romans, "For we are saved by hope."

2. Capitalize the **first word** of each line of a poem.

    Now it is well
    That we should start ("Project" by Mary Fabyan Windeatt)

3. Capitalize **names of individuals, initials, titles** used in direct address or preceding a name, and **titles** describing a family relationship used with a name or in place of a name, but not when the title is preceded by an adjective.

    Lower case: All the moms from the neighborhood came to the play.
    Upper case: Ask Mom if we can go swimming this afternoon.

    Lower case: The priest forgave my sins.
    Upper case: I asked Fr. J.R. Gallagher to say a blessing.

    Lower case: As a paleontologist, you must see a lot of dinosaur bones.
    Upper case: Mr. White, take a look at this dinosaur skeleton!

4. Capitalize all **names** and all **pronouns** that **refer to God**.

    The woman prayed to God that He would heal her son.

5. Capitalize **names** of **ethnic groups, national groups, political parties** and their members, and **languages**.

    Latin   Democrats   Puerto Rican   Greek Orthodox

6. Capitalize names of **organizations, institutions, firms, monuments, bridges, buildings**, and other structures.

    American Life League   George Washington Bridge   the Vatican

7. Capitalize **trade names** and names of **documents** and **laws**.

    Photoshop   *Humanae Vitae*   a Pulitzer Prize   Family Leave Act

HANDBOOK

8. Capitalize **geographical terms** and **regions** or **localities**.

    West Africa   North Vietnam   the Strait of Magellan

9. Capitalize names of **planets** and other heavenly bodies.

    Uranus   the Milky Way   the Big Dipper

    Never capitalize sun or moon, or earth when *earth* is preceded by *the*.

10. Capitalize names of **planes**, **ships**, **trains**, and **spacecraft**.

    the *USS Enterprise*   the *Titanic*   the *Orient Express*

11. Capitalize names of **historic events**, **eras**, **calendar items**, and **most religious terms**.

    the Punic Wars   Christmas Day   the Holy Eucharist

12. Capitalize titles of **literary works**, **works of art**, and **musical compositions**.

    Romeo and Juliet   *The Last Judgment*   *Rhapsody in Blue*
    (by W. Shakepeare)   (by Michelangelo)   (by G. Gershwin)

13. Capitalize **proper adjectives**.

    Catholic religion   Greek alphabet   English literature   Golden Delicious apple

14. Capitalize the **days of the week** and the **month**, but not the seasons.

    Tuesday   Sunday   spring   summer

15. Capitalize **abbreviations** of **proper nouns** and **proper adjectives**.

    U.S.A.   Eng.   U.N.   Am.

HANDBOOK

Punctuation

APOSTROPHE

1. Add an *apostrophe* and an *s* to all singular indefinite pronouns, singular nouns, plural nouns not ending in *s*, and compound nouns to make them possessive. Add only an apostrophe to plural nouns ending in *s* to make them possessive.

   Helen's class   astronauts' uniforms   everyone's grades
   children's games   daughter-in-law's visit
   the Administration's rules

2. If two or more people possess something jointly, use the *possessive form* for the last person's name. If they possess things individually use the possessive form for both names.

   Peter and Paul's apostolate   Louis' and Max's flutes

3. Use the *apostrophe* in place of omitted letters or numbers.

   I'm asking for money.

   I was born in '82.

COLONS AND SEMICOLONS

1. Use a *colon* to introduce a *list* or *to illustrate or restate previous material*:

   There are three theological virtues: faith, hope, and charity.

   By analyzing the history, personality, and teachings of Jesus of Nazareth, we come to one conclusion: Jesus is the Son of God.

2. *Semicolons*, not colons, unite independent clauses. Use the *semicolon* in the following situations:

   a. To separate main clauses not joined by a coordinating conjunction.

      The tomb is empty; Jesus has risen.

Saint Thomas More, Pray for us! J.M.J. English 8 for Young Catholics **173**

HANDBOOK

   b. To separate main clauses joined by a conjunctive adverb or by *for example* or *that is*.

   Jesus ascended into Heaven; nevertheless, we are not alone.

   c. To separate items in a series when those items contain commas.

   Three of the animals most important to the desert dwellers are the dog, for scouting; the horse, for speed and travel; and the camel, for carrying packs.

COMMAS

Use **commas** in the following situations:

1. To separate the main clauses of compound sentences:

   He was the son of Joseph and Mary, but he was also the Son of God.

2. To separate three or more words, phrases, or clauses in a series:

   Water, wine, unleavened bread, and oil constitute the matter of some of the sacraments.

   Note: Other books may tell you it is optional, but we strongly recommend the use of the comma before the *and* in order to avoid any possible confusion between a list of three or more words and an appositive.

3. To separate two or more adjectives preceeding a noun:

   St. Paul was a passionate, intelligent man.

4. To set off parenthetical expressions, nonessential phrases and clauses, direct quotations, and introductory words, phrases, and clauses:

   Parenthetical expression:
   Fishing, of course, is a common metaphor used in the New Testament.

   Nonessential adjectival clause:
   The bridegroom, who is Christ, arrives and finds the women unprepared.

   Nonessential appositive:
   The Bible, the inspired Word of God, has been translated.

HANDBOOK

Introductory adverbial clause:
<u>Before I was baptized</u>, I had despaired of the mercy of God.

Introductory prepositional phrase:
<u>Without any warning</u>, the Lord will descend upon earth.

Direct Quotation:
The boy asked, "<u>Where are you going?</u>".

5. To separate parts of an address and dates:

   145 Heirloom Drive, Longmeadow, MA 02002   December 24, 1627

6. To set off words or phrases of direct address:

   Lord, thank you for your mercy.   How good to see you, Elizabeth!

7. In a friendly letter, after the salutation and the complimentary close:

   Dear Janet,   Your grateful grandson,

DASHES

Use **dashes** to signal a change in thought or to emphasize parenthetical matter. On a typewriter, indicate a dash by using two hyphens.

Kathleen and Raymond will be married this Thursday—three years to the day from when they met.

It's a good idea—many Catholics tend to ignore this sacrament—to go to confession frequently.

ELLIPSIS

Use **ellipsis points** to indicate the omission of material from a quotation. If the omission occurs at the beginning of a sentence, use three spaced points. If the omission occurs in the middle or end, use the correct punctuation (if any), plus three spaced points:

" . . . that all men are created equal; . . . are endowed by their Creator with certain unalienable rights. . . ."

HANDBOOK

HYPHEN

1. Use a hyphen with a fractional number: one-half, three-fourths.
2. Use a hyphen with a compound number: twenty-three chapters, five-hundred people.
3. Use a hyphen with a compound adjective preceding a noun: blue-black bruise; pastel-green dress.
4. Use a hyphen with all *in-laws*: father-in-law, sister-in-law.
5. Use a hyphen with all *great* relatives: great-grandfather.
6. Use a hyphen with all *self* compound words: self-esteem, self-respect.
7. Use a hyphen with all *all* compound words: all-powerful, all-around.
8. Use a hyphen with most *half* compound words: half-asleep.
9. You will notice some words in your reader or dictionary that are spelled with hyphens, though they do not follow a rule: cross-country.

ITALICS (or underline)

1. **Italicize** (or **underline**) titles of books, lengthy poems, plays, films, television series, paintings and sculptures, long musical compositions, court cases, names of newspapers and magazines, ships, trains, airplanes, and spacecraft.

    The House of Seven Gables is a great book.

    or: The House of Seven Gables is a great book.

2. **Italicize** (or **underline**) foreign words and expressions that are not used frequently in English.

    I think you have made a *faux pas*.

3. Italicize words, letters, and numerals used to represent themselves.

    Your password includes the letter *s* and the number *3*.

PARENTHESES

Parentheses set off supplemental material or words that define or explain another word. Punctuate within the parentheses only if the punctuation is part of the parenthetical expression.

HANDBOOK

Noe, one of the forefathers of the Jewish nation (which is probably no older than 5,000 years), trusted God completely.

A *period*, a *question mark*, or an *exclamation point* appears inside the parentheses if it is part of the parenthetical expression, but outside the closing parenthesis if it is part of the sentence.

When St. Peter addressed the crowd (he must have had the gift of tongues!), people from every nation of the earth understood his message.

Did you hear the Pope read the third message (from Fatima)?

PERIODS

1. Use a **period** at the end of an abbreviation. If punctuation other than a period ends the sentence, use both the period and the other punctuation. If the last word of the sentence is an abbreviation, then do not add a second period.

   Can you name the new C.E.O.?
   I have the paints, brushes, boards, etc.

2. Use a period after an initial.

   Robert E. Lee

QUOTATION MARKS

1. Rules guiding the use of **quotation marks**.

   • Always place a comma (,) or period (.) *inside* the closing quotation marks.
   • Always place a colon (:) or semicolon (;) *outside* the closing quotation marks.
   • Place the question mark or exclamation point *inside* the closing quotation marks **when it is part of the quotation**.

   The Pharisees asked, "Who can forgive sins but God alone?"

   • Place the question mark or exclamation point *outside* the closing quotation marks **when it is part of the entire sentence**.

   Why don't you ever listen to me when I remind you that "a penny saved is a penny earned"?

Saint Thomas More, Pray for us!   J.M.J.   English 8 for Young Catholics **177**

HANDBOOK

- If both the sentence and the quotation at the end of the sentence need a question mark (or an exclamation point), use only one punctuation mark and place it inside the closing quotation marks.

    Did you ask, "When did we ever see you naked, Lord, or hungry, or in prison?"

2. **Quotation marks** enclose direct quotations.

    "Once you've seen Fatima," my brother said, "you'll believe in miracles, too."

    At the Last Supper, Christ said, "This is My Body." He did not say, "This symbolizes My Body."

3. Use **single quotation** marks for a quotation within a quotation.

    During the lecture, the professor said, "We must remember, 'Truth exists; the Incarnation happened.'"

4. When writing dialogue, use a new set of **quotation marks** and begin a new paragraph every time the speaker changes.

    "Father?" David asked.
    "Yes, David. How may I help you? Speak up," said Fr. Basil.
    "I want to join the Order of St. John," David boldly declared.

5. Never use **quotation marks** in an indirect quotation (a quotation that does not repeat a person's direct words).

    Correct: Juliet asked, "Romeo, Romeo, wherefore art thou Romeo?" (Exact words)

    Incorrect: Juliet asked, "Why Romeo was named Romeo." (Not exact words)

    Correct: Juliet asked why Romeo was named Romeo. (Not exact words)

HANDBOOK

6. Use **quotation marks** to enclose the titles of short works, such as short stories, short poems, essays, newspaper and magazine articles, book chapters, songs, and single episodes of a television series.

   Short stories: "A Retrieved Reformation" by O. Henry
   Short poems: "Pied Beauty" by G.M. Hopkins
   Essays: "Defense of Poesy" by Sir Philip Sidney
   Articles: "Got Caught Again"
   Chapters: "Soils"
   Songs: "I Can See Clearly Now" by Johnny Nash
   TV episodes: "The Trouble with Tribbles," a Star Trek episode

7. Use **quotation marks** to enclose unfamiliar slang and other unusual or original expressions.

   Every time we went anywhere, Paula had to have her "nuna," a ratty old scarf that gave her comfort.

8. Use **quotation marks** to enclose a definition that is stated directly.

   Rhapsody is a Greek word meaning "to sew songs together."

Abbreviations

For **abbreviations** used in reports, consult your copy of *Composition for Young Catholics*. For a thorough lists of abbreviations, consult the *Chicago Manual of Style*. Abbreviations for books in the Bible can be found in the table of contents of most Bibles. Here are some common abbreviations that you will encounter in your own writing and reading:

a.m.	*ante-meridian* (before noon)
p.m.	*post-meridian* (after noon)
PhD	doctor of philosophy
BC	before Christ
AD	*Anno Domini* (in the year of Our Lord)
ca.	*circa* (about, approximately)
e.g.	*exempli gratia* (for example)
i.e.	*id est* (that is)
etc.	*et cetera* (and so forth)

HANDBOOK

Numbers

1. **Spell out all numbers** through one hundred, those numbers over one hundred that can be written in one or two words, and numbers that occur at the beginning of a sentence.

    I picked three bushels of cherries and two pints of blueberries.

    Approximately three thousand Catholics died in 1943 from Nazi aggression.

    Five thousand college students attended the March for Life last year; 4,300 the year before, and 2,850 the year before that.

2. **Spell out ordinal numbers** (numbers used to indicate order) according to the same rules above. It is also acceptable to use the numeral and the last two letters of the ordinal number; for example, second and third can be rendered as 2nd and 3rd.

    My essay achieved second place in the competition.

    On the 133rd day of his captivity, the prisoner received his fourteenth visitor.

3. **Use numerals** for numbers longer than two words, for money, decimals, precise dates and times, streets and avenues above ten, and all house, apartment, and room numbers.

    I told him three times that I live at 27 Cardinal Street, Apartment 5.

4. Express all **related numbers in a sentence as numerals** if any one should be expressed as a numeral.

    The Rosary procession grew from 10 to 25 in the first hour, then from 25 to 150 before we finished three hours later.

5. **Spell out numbers** that express time *without* a.m. or p.m., centuries, decades, and streets and avenues of less than ten.

    one o'clock   twenty-first century   the eighties   Fifth Street

CREDITS

List of Illustrations and Artists

Page	Title	Artist
1	Catherine of Alexandria	Raphael
2	Benedict	Champaigne
3	Holy Family with Cousins	Batoni
5	Christ Holding the Eucharist	Juanes
14	Madonna and Child	Raphael
16	Madonna and Child	Ittenbach
18	Madonna della Seggiola	Sanzio Raffaello
24	Last Supper	Champ
25	Last Supper	Flandes
29	Christ with a Child	Bloch
30	Christ and the Centurion	Boullogne
31	Charles Borromeo	Guercino
32	Christ Leaving the Praetorium	Doré
40	Christ with a Reed	Megnard
56	St. Anthony of Padua	Leal
57	Our Lady Intercedes for the Souls in Purgatory	Champaigne
58	Annunciation	Master of Moulins
59	Last Supper	Rosselli
62	Madonna of the Eucharist	Ingres
68	Mary the Spinner	Feliks Cichocki - Nałęcz
74	Finding in the Temple	Holman Hunt
78	Stoning of Saint Stephen	Rubens
79	Conversion of Saint Paul	Caravaggio

CREDITS

Page	Title	Artist
80	Paul and Barnabas at Lystra	Corneille
81	Paul	Champaigne
87	Peter and John Heal the Lame Man	Poussin
113	David and Goliath	Polish 19th century
114	Joan of Arc	Stilke
115	Christ Drives out the Money Changers	Jordaens
118	Christ Jesus	El Greco
120	Angel of the Annunciation	Champaigne
129	Anthony and the Starving Donkey	Van Dyck
130	Assumption	Champaigne
131	Supper at Emmaus	Overbeck
137	Good Shepherd	Champaigne
138	Good Shepherd	Portana
148	Peter Repents	Seghers
150	Maximillian Kolbe	Unknown
151	Assumption	Vouet
152	Cecilia	Paelinck Horgnies
153	Cana	Murillo
155	Joseph	Honthorst
159	Blessed Mother Meditating	Cope
163	Madonna and Child	Dyce
170	Saint Cecilia	Delaroche
177	Madonna and Child	Murillo

ANSWER KEY

ANSWER KEY FOR PRACTICE EXERCISES

Exercise 1 Proper nouns should be circled in the exercise.

1. proper nouns: God, Adam, Eve
common noun: <u>parents</u>

2. proper noun: Jesus
common nouns: <u>men</u>, <u>apostles</u>

3. proper nouns: Gabriel, Mary, Our Lord
common nouns: <u>angel</u>, <u>mother</u>

4. proper nouns: Jesus Christ, God
common nouns: <u>sins</u>, <u>children</u>

5. proper nouns: John, Jesus, Jordan River
common nouns: <u>cousin</u>, <u>believers</u>

6. proper nouns: St. John, Jesus
common noun: <u>river</u>

7. proper noun: Holy Land
common nouns: <u>pilgrimage</u>, <u>experience</u>

8. No proper nouns
common nouns: <u>priesthood</u>, <u>vocation</u>

9. proper noun: Holy Redeemer Church
common nouns: <u>choir</u>, <u>state</u>

10. proper noun: Sunday
common nouns: <u>choir</u>, <u>days</u>

Exercise 2

1. congregation
2. club
3. Society or Immaculate Conception Society
4. crowd, orchestra
5. audience, band
6. mankind
7. teams, League or National Football League
8. jury
9. community
10. Confederacy or Confederacy of American States
11. herds
12. congregation
13. board
14. crew
15. flock

Exercise 3

1. Mother Teresa, sympathy, poor, encouragement, sick
2. Christ, state, grace, happiness
3. Courage, times, grace, God
4. examples, faith, Gospels
5. words, Jesus, joy, hope, hearts
6. children knowledge, laws, God, duty, parents
7. Anger, love, evil, good
8. marriage, man, woman, sickness, health
9. Elizabeth Ann Seton, truthfulness, Faith
10. perseverance, general

Exercise 4

1. 3
2. 1, 3
3. 2, 3, 1
4. 1, 3, 2
5. 2, 3
6. 2, 3, 3
7. 1, 3
8. 2, 3
9. 2, 3, 1
10. 2, 1, 3

Exercise 5A

1. radios
2. herds
3. sheep
4. Xs
5. 1960s
6. colonies
7. flamingos (or flamingoes)
8. mouse
9. tomato
10. leaves
11. The Mrs. Grants
12. crucifix
13. Tuesdays
14. chiefs
15. sisters-in-law
16. goose
17. moose
18. mathematics
19. lieutenants
20. Chinese

Exercise 5B

1. blessings
2. onyxes
3. Masses
4. mouthfuls
5. trout
6. donkeys
7. 1000s
8. dozens
9. halves
10. staffs
11. icons
12. attorneys general
13. women
14. ladies
15. patios
16. jigsaws
17. corpses
18. crops
19. corps
20. kimonos

Exercise 6

1. F
2. M
3. N
4. M
5. M
6. F
7. F
8. N
9. N
10. M
11. N
12. F
13. M
14. F
15. N
16. N
17. N
18. M
19. F
20. M
21. M
22. N
23. M
24. M
25. M
26. N
27. M
28. M
29. M
30. F

Exercise 7

1. martyrs
2. St. Peter
3. Jesus
4. Scribes, Pharisees
5. widow
6. apostles
7. Jesus
8. News
9. you, David
10. class

ANSWER KEY

Exercise 8
1. traveler
2. virtue
3. leader
4. Immanuel, "God-is-with-us"
5. Savior
6. sin, matter

Exercise 9
1. Mary
2. Lord
3. Lord
4. Joseph
5. Teacher
6. Jerusalem
7. Carol
8. Death

Exercise 10 The words in bold should be underlined and circled.
1. Fortitude, **virtue**, firmness, difficulties, constancy, pursuit, good
2. Pope St. Leo, **Doctor**, Church, Attila, Rome
3. ships, **Nina**, **Pinta**, **Santa Maria**, East Indies
4. Dominic Savio, **student**, St. John Bosco, teenager
5. founder, sodality, Fr. Jones, **pastor**
6. Mesopotamia, **land**, kings, prosperity
7. John Paul II, **pontiff**, justice, freedom, world

Exercise 11
1. Christopher
2. Guardian Angel
3. souls
4. path
5. pile

Exercise 12A
1. Baptism (S), sacrament (SC)
2. Confirmation (S), sacrament (AP)
3. Confession (E)
4. God (DA)
5. apostles (S), priests (AP), bishops (AP), men (SC)
6. Jesus (S)
7. apostles (S)
8. Mary (DA), mother (AP)
9. Jesus (S)
10. Simon Peter (S), fisherman (SC)

Exercise 12B
1. Peter / you | are \ rock

2. Jesus (Savior) | loves | us / our

Exercise 13A
1. priest's, priests'
2. fox's, foxes'
3. baby's, babies'
4. sister-in-law's, sisters-in-law's
5. altar boy's, altar boys'
6. city's, cities'
7. mouse's, mice's
8. pope's, popes'
9. gentleman's, gentlemen's
10. Catholic's, Catholics'
11. moose's, moose's
12. patio's, patios'
13. chair's, chairs'
14. queen's, queens'
15. wife's, wives'
16. child's, children's
17. Mrs. Finch's, the Mrs. Finches'
18. turkey's, turkeys'
19. potato's, potatoes'
20. cliff's, cliffs'

Exercise 13B
1. Martha, Mary's
2. Judas', Peter's
3. boys, girls'
4. brother's and sister's
5. Paula's, Rose's
6. Anthony's, Paul's
7. directors, singers'
8. Adam, Eve's

Exercise 14
1. resentment
2. Temple
3. Jesus
4. way
5. Cuba

Exercise 15A
1. rain
2. mail
3. ride
4. drawing
5. saying

Exercise 15B
1. deacon
2. Holy Innocents
3. The Oratory
4. treasurer
5. cardinal

ANSWER KEY

Exercise 16
1. days
2. half-hour
3. minutes
4. miles
5. feet

Exercise 17
1. Jesus
2. Mary
3. Mother Teresa
4. lepers
5. seminary
6. children
7. children
8. aunt
9. sister

Exercise 18
1. Boston, visitors, city
2. shrine, frame, rays
3. crutches, canes, side, altar
4. cures, shrine
5. stops, Boston
6. summer, buses, Haymarket Square
7. crowd, Faneuil Hall, legislature
8. visit, Old North Church
9. church, stairs, tower, British
10. souvenirs, bags, God, blessings

Exercise 19
1. Father
2. martyr
3. precursor
4. nun
5. program

Exercise 20 Words in bold should be circled.
1. **us**, first, plural, masculine
   He, third, singular, masculine
2. **he**, third, singular, masculine
   you, second, plural, masculine
3. **me**, first, singular, masculine
   I, first, singular, masculine
4. **I**, first, singular, masculine
   you, second, plural, masculine
   He, third, singular, masculine
   you, second, plural, masculine
5. **you**, second, singular, feminine
6. **You**, second, singular, feminine
   Him, third, singular, masculine
7. **He**, third, singular, masculine
8. **He**, third, singular, masculine
   her, third, singular, feminine
9. **Me**, first, singular, masculine
   I, first, singular, masculine
   you, second, plural, masculine
10. **He**, third, singular, masculine
    them, third, plural, masculine

Exercise 21A
1. They, I
2. we
3. she
4. we, they, he
5. he
6. They, we
7. we
8. they
9. They
10. We
11. they
12. he
13. We
14. I
15. he

Exercise 21B
1.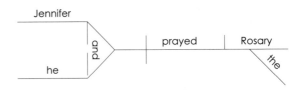
2.

Exercise 22
1. us (DO), us (OP)
2. us (DO)
3. them (IO)
4. Him (OP)
5. her (IO)
6. him (DO)
7. her (DO), her (DO)
8. us (IO)
9. me (OP)
10. them (DO)
11. Me (DO)
12. her (IO), Him (OP)
13. Him (DO)
14. her (DO)
15. her (DO)
16. them (DO)
17. her (OP)
18. her (OP)
19. me (IO)
20. me (DO), me (DO)

ANSWER KEY

Exercise 23
1. I
2. we
3. she
4. they
5. he
6. him
7. he
8. I
9. she
10. they
11. she
12. I
13. we
14. they
15. they

Exercise 24A Words in bold should be circled.
1. **Himself**, intensive
2. **ourselves**, intensive
3. **ourselves**, reflexive
4. **Himself**, intensive
5. **itself**, intensive
6. **ourselves**, reflexive
7. **herself**, reflexive
8. **himself**, intensive
9. **himself**, intensive
10. **themselves**, reflexive
11. **ourselves**, intensive
12. **themselves**, reflexive
13. **themselves**, reflexive
14. **ourselves**, reflexive
15. **Himself**, intensive

Exercise 24B
1.

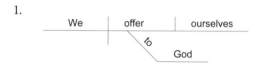

2.

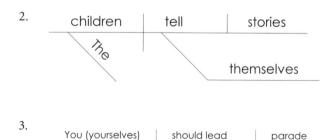

3.

Exercise 25A
1. ours, indirect object
2. Mine, subject
3. yours, direct object
4. his, direct object
5. yours, object of a preposition
6. theirs, subjective complement
7. yours, subject
8. theirs, indirect object
9. ours, subject
10. yours, object of a preposition

Exercise 25B
1.

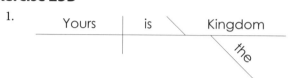

2.

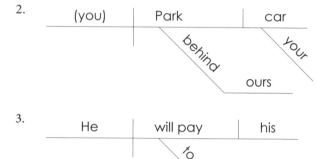

3.

Exercise 26A
1. adjective
2. pronoun
3. adjective
4. pronoun
5. pronoun
6. adjective
7. adjective
8. pronoun
9. pronoun
10. adjective

Exercise 26B Words in bold should be circled.
1. **these**, subjective complement
2. **those**, object of a preposition
3. **this**, subject
4. **those**, indirect object
5. **that**, object of a preposition
6. **This**, subject
7. **that**, direct object
8. **these**, subjective complement
9. **these**, indirect object
10. **those**, direct object

Exercise 27A Words in bold should be circled.
1. **Who**, subject, nominative
2. **what**, object of a preposition, objective
3. **What**, subject, nominative
4. **What**, direct object, objective
5. **whom**, object of a preposition, objective
6. **Which**, direct object, objective
7. **Who**, subject, nominative

ANSWER KEY

8. **Whose**, direct object, objective
9. **What**, subject, nominative
10. **What**, subject, nominative
11. **Who**, subject, nominative
12. **Which**, subject, nominative
13. **whom**, object of a preposition, objective
14. **Who**, subject, nominative
15. **Who**, subject, nominative
16. **Whom**, object of a preposition, objective
17. **Which**, subject, nominative
18. **Who**, subject, nominative
19. **What**, subject, nominative
20. **Whom**, direct object, objective

Exercise 27B

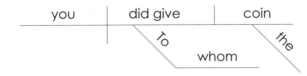

Exercise 28 Words in bold should be circled.

1. **Who**, One, subject, nominative
2. **Who**, Son, subject, nominative
3. **which**, name, subject, nominative
4. **Whom**, Jesus, direct object, objective
5. **which**, date, object of a preposition, objective
6. **that**, road, subject, nominative
7. **which**, house, object of a preposition, objective
8. **that**, man, subject, nominative
9. **Whom**, One, object of a preposition, objective
10. **whom**, woman, direct object, objective
11. **which**, Jerusalem, subject, nominative
12. **Whom**, Son, object of a preposition, objective
13. **whom**, cousin, direct object, objective
14. **which**, story, direct object, objective
15. **that**, people, subject, nominative

Exercise 29A

1. wish
2. needs
3. needs
4. are
5. is
6. reaches
7. are
8. arrives
9. stays
10. appeals
11. arrive, is
12. are
13. cheers
14. is

Exercise 29B

1. him
2. he
3. it
4. them
5. him
6. they
7. they
8. she
9. him
10. them

Exercise 29C

1. his
2. their
3. his
4. his
5. their
6. his
7. his
8. their
9. their
10. his

Exercise 30

1. wealthy C
2. Roman P
3. sick C, back C
4. Slav P
5. old C, beautiful C
6. chocolate C, large C, white C
7. vivid C, Irish P
8. rich C
9. deaf C, frozen C
10. loud C, gentle C

Exercise 31

1. narrow AA, wide SC
2. holy, OC
3. omnipotent SC, omniscient SC
4. grassy AA, tranquil AA
5. solid AA, firm OC
6. excellent OC
7. colorful AA, vast AA
8. radiant SC, resplendent AA, blue AA, white AA
9. happy SC, troubled SC
10. Poor AA, difficult OC

Exercise 32

1. An, the, the, the
2. The, the , the
3. The, two, an, a, the, twelve
4. The, four, an, the, seventeenth
5. the, first, a

Exercise 33

1. Adjective
2. Adjective
3. Pronoun
4. Adjective
5. Adjective
6. Pronoun
7. Pronoun
8. Adjective

ANSWER KEY

Exercise 34A
1. that
2. these
3. this
4. These
5. this

Exercise 34B
1. This
2. this
3. these
4. Those
5. those

Exercise 34C
1. these A, those P
2. those P, this A
3. these A, those P
4. This P, that A
5. These A, that P

Exercise 34D

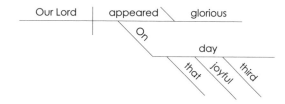

Exercise 35A
1. My
2. Their
3. our
4. your
5. our, your
6. our
7. My, our
8. their
9. its
10. his, her

Exercise 35B

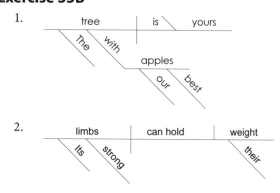

Exercise 36
1. What
2. which
3. which
4. what
5. whose

Exercise 37
1. parent
2. churches
3. time
4. oil
5. mother
6. times
7. apparition
8. intentions
9. juice
10. boy

Exercise 38
1. drier, driest
2. more / less thoughtful, most / least thoughtful
3. better, best
4. more / less knowledgeable, most / least knowledgeable
5. NONE, NONE
6. fancier, fanciest
7. more, most
8. worse, worst
9. NONE, NONE
10. more, most

Exercise 39
1. fewer
2. less
3. fewer
4. less
5. less
6. fewer
7. Fewer, less
8. Fewer
9. less
10. fewer
11. fewer
12. fewer
13. less
14. less
15. less

Exercise 40
1. the
2. the
3. —
4. the
5. the
6. —
7. —
8. a
9. —
10. the
11. the
12. the
13. the

ANSWER KEY

14. a
15. —

Exercise 41

1. noun
2. adjective
3. noun
4. noun
5. noun
6. adjective
7. adjective
8. noun
9. adjective
10. adjective
11. adjective
12. noun

Exercise 42

There should be a check mark before items 1, 3, 6, 8, 10, 11, 12, 13, 15, and 19.

There is no exercise for Lesson 43.

Exercise 44

1. lived; have, has, had lived
2. explained; have, has, had explained
3. tripped; have, has, had tripped
4. delayed; have, has, had delayed
5. adored; have, has, had adored
6. blessed; have, has, had blessed
7. composed; have, has, had composed
8. diagrammed; have, has, had diagrammed
9. remembered; have, has, had remembered
10. started; have, has, had started

Exercise 45

1. rode
2. known
3. taught
4. fought
5. lit or lighted
6. sought
7. come
8. sank
9. wrote
10. sang
11. sung
12. known
13. knelt
14. laid
15. found
16. seen
17. went
18. did
19. made
20. chosen

Exercise 46

1. rise
2. raised, Lazarus
3. laid, life
4. lies
5. laid, body
6. laid, scapulars
7. lay
8. rise
9. lie
10. lays, baby
11. risen; rose
12. raised, curtain
13. laid, foundation
14. risen
15. Lie; lay, head

Exercise 47

1. accepted, T
2. spread, I
3. have fought, T
4. worked, I
5. were killed, T
6. flourished, I
7. survived, I
8. was taken, T
9. worked, T
10. spoke, I
11. was founded, T
12. developed, I
13. was grown, T
14. melted, I
15. joined, T
16. chose, T
17. develops, T
18. was kicked, T
19. went, I
20. hastened, I

Exercise 48A Words in bold should be circled.

1. **was**, Simeon (S), prophet (SC)
2. **was**, prophet (S), well-known (SC)
3. **are**, Faith (S), hope (S), charity (S), virtues (SC)
4. **is**, virtue (S), charity (SC)
5. **felt**, man (S), virtuous (SC)
6. **has remained**, Church (S), faithful (SC)
7. **can remain**, None (S), indifferent (SC)
8. **was**, mother (S), St. Silvia (SC)
9. **became**, monastery (S), home (SC)
10. **became**, St. Benedict (S), leader (SC)

Exercise 48B

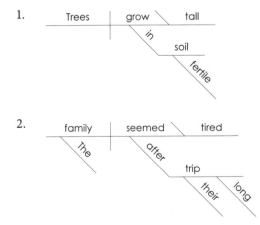

ANSWER KEY

3.
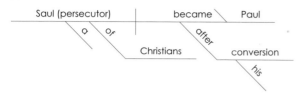

Exercise 49A

1. Mother Teresa helped the poor people of Calcutta.
2. The Magi laid gold, frankincense, and myrrh near the manger.
3. In Denver, the Holy Father was met by Dr. Clark.
4. Slave traders took St. Patrick to Ireland.
5. Jesus turned the water into wine at the wedding of Cana.
6. The feet of His apostles were washed by Jesus.
7. Lazarus was raised from the dead by Jesus.
8. Pope John Paul II was succeeded by Pope Benedict XVI.

Exercise 49B

1.
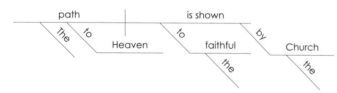

2.
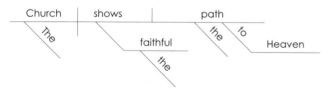

Exercise 50A

1. feared, past
2. intensifies, present
3. was elected, past
4. will be held, future
5. enacted, past
6. are spoken, present
7. forgot, past
8. will hear, future
9. Give, present; will kill, future
10. stepped, past
11. were killed, past; will join, future

Exercise 50B

1. use, present
2. will speak, future
3. learn, present
4. look, present
5. was built, past
6. will have, future
7. had, past
8. were written, past
9. understood, past
10. said, past

Exercise 50C

1. ran, past
2. caught, past
3. go, present
4. raised, past
5. will read, future
6. chosen, past
7. led, future
8. ring, present
9. keep, future
10. spoken, past

Exercise 51A Words in bold should be circled.

1. **have prepared**, present perfect
2. **will have finished**, future perfect
3. **had written**, past perfect
4. **has produced**, present perfect
5. **have kept**, present perfect
6. **had finished**, past perfect
7. **will have fallen**, future perfect

Exercise 51B

1. you have thrown, you had thrown, you will have thrown
2. they have forgotten, they had forgotten, they will have forgotten
3. it has sunk, it had sunk, it will have sunk
4. we have ridden, we had ridden, we will have ridden
5. he has shaken, he had shaken, he will have shaken
6. you have laid, you had laid, you will have laid
7. she has led, she had led, she will have led

Exercise 51C

1. had used
2. will have forgiven
3. have learned
4. had been converted
5. will have known
6. will have nailed
7. had arrested
8. will have finished
9. have taught
10. have crucified

There is no exercise for Lesson 52

ANSWER KEY

Exercise 53
1. does
2. will have been conquered
3. wept
4. has been prepared
5. will speak
6. had been fed
7. was baptized
8. preferred
9. will be bound
10. has protected

Exercise 54
1. A, Emphatic
2. A, Potential
3. A, Emphatic
4. A, Emphatic
5. P, Potential
6. A, Progressive
7. A, Potential
8. P, Progressive
9. A, Emphatic
10. A, Potential
11. A, Potential
12. P, Progressive
13. A, Potential
14. P, Potential
15. A, Progressive
16. A, Emphatic
17. P, Potential
18. P, Progressive
19. A, Potential
20. A, Progressive

Exercise 55
1. Be
2. glorify
3. Love
4. Keep
5. Go, preach, tell
6. Consider
7. Keep, listen

Exercise 56 Words in bold should be circled.
1. vocation, **is**, third, singular
2. Pope John Paul II, **has named**, third, singular
3. prelates, **are**, third, plural
4. names **will remain**, third, plural
5. group, ours, **must speak**, third, plural
6. food, supplies, **were assembled**, third, plural
7. People, **have been sharing**, third, plural
8. pastor, mayor, **are amazed**, third, plural
9. Everyone, **is**, third, singular
10. None, **are**, third, plural
11. Water, food, clothing, **have been distributed**, third, plural
12. storm, **will pass**, third, singular; they, **will rebuild**, third, plural

Exercise 57A
1. say, is
2. has
3. remains
4. is
5. is
6. start
7. have
8. have

Exercise 57B
1. serves
2. is
3. suffices
4. are
5. is
6. wears
7. are
8. do
9. are
10. are
11. are
12. participates

Exercise 58
1. have
2. forgives
3. were
4. are
5. shows
6. lets
7. was
8. share
9. was
10. was
11. take
12. attends
13. learn
14. are
15. was

Exercise 59
1. has
2. looks
3. is
4. brings
5. brings
6. is
7. Is
8. receives
9. spends
10. goes
11. reminds
12. is
13. leads
14. has
15. is

Exercise 60
1. is
2. was
3. were
4. were
5. were
6. was

ANSWER KEY

7. lead
8. leads
9. has
10. have

Exercise 61

1. has
2. was
3. wins
4. arrives
5. is
6. was
7. performs
8. sings
9. leave
10. was
11. is
12. were
13. was
14. submits
15. has

Exercise 62

1. Noun
2. Noun
3. Verb
4. Verb
5. Noun
6. Verb
7. Verb
8. Noun
9. Noun
10. Verb
11. Verb
12. Verb
13. Noun
14. Verb

There is no exercise for Lesson 63.

Exercise 64A

1. frequently
2. very, quickly
3. upward
4. truly, unusually
5. barely
6. there, authoritatively
7. always, too, fast
8. merely
9. suddenly, extremely
10. Inside, mercifully
11. readily
12. promptly
13. gratefully
14. Majestically, back
15. aside

Exercise 64B

1.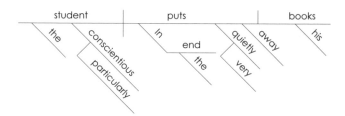

2.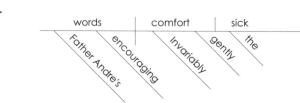

Exercise 65

1. any
2. no one
3. ever
4. anyone
5. any
6. any
7. Never
8. any

Exercise 66

1. how
2. Where
3. When
4. Why
5. When
6. How
7. How

Exercise 67 Answers will vary. Some possible answers are provided here.

1. pounds
2. feet
3. dollars
4. days, weeks, months
5. inches, feet
6. way
7. pounds
8. morning, afternoon, evening, week

Exercise 68

1. more/less quickly, most/least quickly
2. little, least
3. foolishly, more/less foolishly
4. later, latest
5. better, best
6. loudly, most/least loudly
7. NONE
8. soon, sooner

ANSWER KEY

9. much, most
10. courteously, more/less courteously
11. NONE
12. faster, fastest
13. often, most/least often
14. worse, worst
15. more/less readily; most/least readily
16. eagerly, more/less eagerly
17. high, highest
18. NONE
19. far, farther
20. safe, safer

Exercise 69A Words in bold should be circled.

1. **seriously**, studies
2. **quiet**, voice
3. **patiently**, taught
4. **sensible**, answer
5. **solidly**, was built
6. **comfortably**, is sleeping
7. **simply**, was dressed

Exercise 69B Words in bold should be circled.

1. The young skater fell **hard** upon the hard ice, but he **hardly** felt it through his thick snowsuit.
2. Fran knew **little** about the cloistered nuns, but she cared **enough** to learn more details.
3. His last homily did **not** last **long**, but it **definitely** made a lasting impression.
4. Tommy could **not** be **still** through the entire movie, but he remembers it **still**.
5. "**No**," he **vehemently** said, "I will **not ever** deny You, Lord!"
6. **Why** does the slow snail **slowly** glide the width of the path to the long grass **beyond**?

Exercise 69C Answers will vary. Some possible answers are provided here.

1. skillfully, expertly
2. reverently, well
3. small, strong
4. sweet, strong
5. carefully, intently
6. thoroughly, truly

Exercise 69D

1.
2.

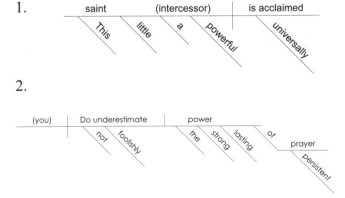

Exercise 70

1. sad
2. mercifully
3. kindly
4. charitable
5. radiant
6. calm
7. certain
8. surely
9. poorly
10. softly

Exercise 71

1. farther
2. further
3. further
4. farther
5. farther
6. further
7. further
8. farther
9. farther
10. further

Exercise 72A

1. against, VERB
2. with, NOUN
3. Besides, VERB
4. from, VERB
5. of, NOUN
6. under, VERB
7. on, NOUN
8. on, NOUN
9. at, VERB
10. in, VERB
11. of, NOUN
12. To, VERB
13. of, NOUN

Exercise 72B

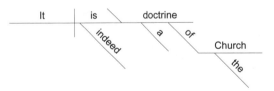

Exercise 73

1. adverb
2. adverb
3. preposition
4. adverb
5. adverb
6. adverb
7. preposition
8. preposition
9. adverb
10. preposition

ANSWER KEY

Exercise 74A
1. besides
2. among
3. beside
4. between
5. beside
6. besides
7. among
8. between
9. besides
10. among

Exercise 74B

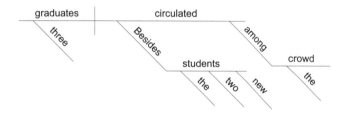

Exercise 75A
1. from
2. into
3. into
4. into
5. off
6. from
7. into
8. from
9. off
10. into

Exercise 75B

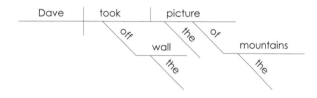

Exercise 76
1. with
2. with
3. from
4. with
5. with
6. at
7. from
8. from
9. at
10. from
11. from
12. with

Exercise 77
1. from the woods, ADV
2. to a high mountain, ADV; before them, ADV
3. to a cross, ADV; for our sins, ADV
4. for us, ADV; at the hour, ADV; of our death, ADJ
5. behind the altar, ADV
6. under his clothes, ADV
7. At the age, ADV; of fifteen, ADJ

There is no exercise for Lesson 78.

Exercise 79A Words in bold should be circled.
1. Answer is provided.
2. **and**, brave determined, subjective complements
3. **and**, inspired, encouraged, predicates
4. **and**, hardship, famine, direct objects
5. **not only, but also**, Anne, Angela, subjects
6. **neither, nor**, sinned, desired, predicates
7. **either, or**, priest, brother, subjective complements
8. **Both, and**, prayer, works, subjects
9. **but**, lost, gained, predicates
10. **and**, Tom and Michael, indirect objects

Exercise 79B Words in bold should be circled.
1. Answer is provided.
2. **but**, in the summer, on rainy days, ADV
3. **but**, with lapels, without buttons, ADJ
4. **either, or** to Baltimore, to Washington, ADV
5. **or**, around the lake, on the mountain trail, ADJ
6. **both, and**, for the proposition, against it, ADJ
7. **and**, to the pier, around it, ADV
8. **and**, for priests, for missionaries, ADJ
9. **but**, with milk, without sugar, ADJ
10. **either, or**, from the Bible, from a spiritual book, ADV

Exercise 80A Words in bold should be circled.
1. **and** You (S), must take (P); they (S), must abide (P)
2. **either, or** Mary (S), will go (P); she (S); will stay (P)
3. **but**, children (S), told (P); people (S) did believe (P)
4. **but**, I (S), would play (P); I (S), must study (P)
5. **and**, shoes (S), are (P); they (S) do fit (P)
6. **neither, nor,** They (S), listened (P); obeyed (P)
7. **or**, I (S), should leave (P); I (S), will be (P)
8. **but**, she (S), wanted (P); she (S), decided (P)
9. **and**, Helen (S), will do (P); she (S), will study (P)
10. **and**, Danny (S), will play (P); Myra (S), will accompany (P)

Exercise 80B
9.

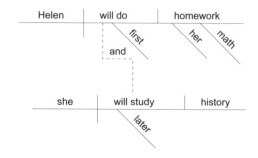

10.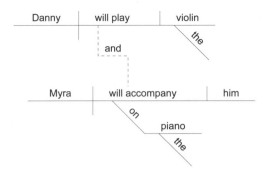

Exercise 82B

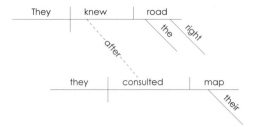

Exercise 81A (Words in bold should be circled.)

1. I love to attend Mass **because I can receive Jesus in Holy Communion**.
2. We will clean the house **so Mom can rest**.
3. We will do our chores now **so that we may play basketball later**.
4. We shall have a Rosary procession **provided that it does not rain**.
5. **Although she is busy**, she finds time to help the sick.
6. **If they became engaged**, we would plan for the wedding.
7. We homeschool **so that we may become well educated in the Catholic Faith**.
8. **Although Jesus worked many miracles**, some leaders rejected Him.
9. Mom will take us to the zoo today **provided that we clean our room**.
10. **Because so many people came to the novena**, Father heard Confessions.
11. **Unless there is a Holy Hour on Friday night**, we shall go to the movies.
12. The children helped their grandmother clean the house **as if it were their own home**.

Exercise 81B

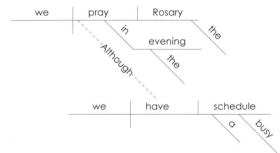

Exercise 82A (Words in bold should be circled.)

1. **nevertheless**, coordinate
2. **until**, subordinate
3. **before**, subordinate
4. **however**, coordinate
5. **While**, subordinate
6. **consequently**, coordinate
7. **When**, subordinate
8. **where**, subordinate
9. **therefore**, coordinate
10. **however**, coordinate

Exercise 83

1. as if
2. as
3. Like
4. as
5. as if
6. like
7. as if
8. as
9. like
10. like
11. As
12. like

Exercise 84

1. Look! Hooray!
2. Oh
3. Hush!
4. Excellent!
5. Bravo!
6. Alleluia, Alleluia! Alleluia!
7. Oh
8. Wow!
9. Say!
10. Well

Exercise 85

1. If you take the time to pray about it, you (S), take (P), you (S), will make (P)
2. After the angel appeared to him in a dream, angel (S), appeared (P), Joseph (S), left (P)
3. Whatever you do, you (S), do (P), it (S), must be (P)
4. that the Trinity is a mystery, it (S), is (P), Trinity (S), is (P)
5. while others are cloistered, nuns (S), work (P), others (S), are (P)
6. which Mother Teresa recited every day, prayer, (S), Mother Teresa, (S), recited (P), soothes (P)
7. Whether or not he planned it that way, he (S), planned (P), he (S), arrived (P)
8. how we may obtain sanctifying grace, Father Martin (S), explained (P), we (S), may obtain (P)
9. that He would send His only Son, God (S), kept (P), He (S), would send (P)
10. Unless we notify you otherwise, we (S), notify (P), Mass (S), will be held (P)
11. which is the capital of the United States, Washington DC (S), which (S), is (P), welcomes (P)
12. why he decided to go to Chicago for the weekend, He (S), did say (P), he (S), decided (P)

ANSWER KEY

Exercise 86A Words in bold should be circled.
1. **St. John Lateran** which is one of the many churches in Rome
2. **chapel** where the Eucharist is perpetually exposed
3. **Children** who are disciplined
4. **saint** who explained the doctrine of Transubstantiation
5. **Pantheon** which was a pagan temple
6. **St. Peter** who was martyred in 64 A. D.
7. **people** who anxiously awaited the arrival of the pope
8. **People** who travel to Lourdes
9. **church** that can trace its beginning to Jesus Christ
10. **one** that completely removes the punishment of sin
11. **Paris** which is the most famous city in France
12. **St. Jane de Chantal** who founded the Visitation Sisters
13. **part** that proclaims the Church's central beliefs
14. **book** that contains all the readings for the Mass
15. **storm** that frightened the disciples

Exercise 86B

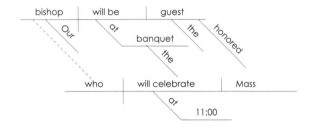

Exercise 87A Words in bold should be circled.
1. **answered**, because she loved God
2. **is known**, Since the pope seemed trapped at Avignon
3. **left**, when the Mass was over
4. **should make**, When you visit Rome
5. **stopped**, where the money was buried
6. **held**, As if her life depended on it
7. **thought**, after the fish had swallowed him
8. **is occupied**, if the red light is on
9. **may enter**, When the green light is on above the confessional
10. **will drive**, because he missed the bus
11. **knew**, When I smelled incense
12. **will visit**, after I finish saying the Rosary
13. **reached**, because he could run faster than Peter
14. **stayed**, until the parade ended
15. **will complete**, Because you have paid attention

Exercise 87B

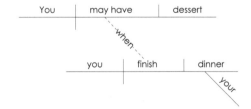

Exercise 88A
1. What God tells us in the Bible, S
2. Whatever caused the outburst, S
3. that He arose from the dead, SC
4. that they pick up their toys, A
5. that souls will be saved, SC
6. that so many people have been cured at Lourdes, A
7. That St. Peter was the first pope, S
8. that the president should be a good moral leader, SC
9. What keeps us in God's grace, S
10. that your brother has been ordained a priest, A
11. that God became man, A
12. why the rich young man walked away, SC
13. Whoever keeps my commandments, S
14. that Christ will come again, SC
15. that the pope has written a new encyclical, A

Exercise 88B

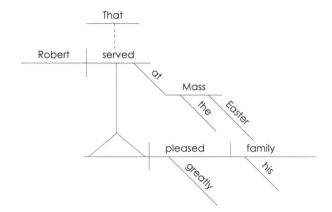

Exercise 88C
1. that there have been thousands of miracles, DO
2. whoever wants one, IO
3. what Father Damien did for the lepers, OP
4. that Christ died for the salvation of our souls, DO
5. that He would send a Redeemer, DO
6. what the priest told them, OP
7. whoever asks for them, OP
8. whatever needs it, IO
9. what they saw at Lourdes, OP
10. that we should pray the Rosary, DO
11. where you sit, OP
12. whoever needs them, IO
13. that he must save his child, OP
14. that virtue is a habit of the soul, DO
15. that everyone must receive the sacraments, DO

ANSWER KEY

Exercise 88D

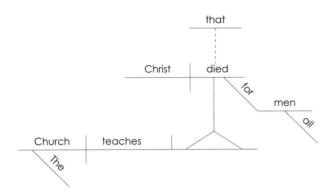

Exercise 89A Words in bold should be circled.

1. **St. Matthew and St. Mark** wrote Gospels.
2. **The apostles** evangelized and baptized many people.
3. **Sloth**, **envy**, and **greed** are three of the seven cardinal sins.
4. **A group of girls** entered the convent.
5. **The search for the true Cross** spread and lasted hundreds of years.
6. **A vine-covered abbey** stood on top of the hill.
7. **three purple candles and one pink one**, During Advent, are placed in a wreath.
8. **The baby** gurgled and cooed at his father.
9. **we** After Mass, should thank and adore Our Lord.
10. **Today** is the first day of summer.
11. **Mary and her little sister, Agnes,** knelt and prayed for the soul of their grandmother.
12. **Sacraments** are the means to sanctifying grace.
13. **The third Gospel in the Bible and the Acts of the Apostles** were written by St. Luke.
14. **Priests and bishops** instruct and lead the faithful.
15. **The priest** acts as a mediator between God and man.

Exercise 89B

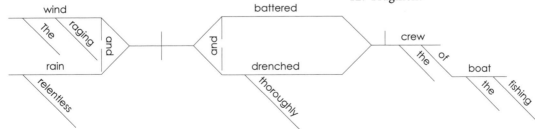

Exercise 90 Words in bold should be circled.

1. **You** can receive many graces by going to Mass, natural
2. Did **you** hear the great news, inverted
3. **Some people** prefer a quiet life, natural
4. Arched over the hills is **a beautiful rainbow**, inverted
5. Below a cliff runs **a swirling river**, inverted
6. High above us, **puffy white clouds** passed by, natural
7. Here is **a book from the library**, inverted
8. **Who** will attend the conference, natural
9. By their works **you** will know them, natural
10. On the trapeze sat **the circus clown**, inverted

Exercise 91

1. declarative, .
2. interrogative, ?
3. declarative, .
4. exclamatory, !
5. interrogative, ?
6. imperative, .
7. imperative, .
8. imperative, . OR exclamatory, !
9. exclamatory, !
10. declarative, .
11. exclamatory, !
12. declarative, .

Exercise 92

1. simple
2. simple
3. compound
4. complex
5. complex
6. compound
7. simple
8. simple
9. compound
10. complex
11. complex
12. simple

Exercise 93

1. Complete
2. Fragment
3. Complete
4. Complete
5. Run-on
6. Complete
7. Fragment
8. Run-on
9. Fragment
10. Complete
11. Complete
12. Fragment

NOTES